Hi I NEED A MIRACLE!

HOW TO PRAY AND RECEIVE ONE!

BY
JUDY O'HALLORAN

A STORY THAT WILL BRING HOPE AND ENCOURAGEMENT TO THOSE WHO ARE IN CRISIS. THE MESSAGE IS,
"LEARN TO PRAY, AND DON'T GIVE UP!"

Copyright © 2014 by Judy O'Halloran
HELP! I NEED A MIRACLE!
HOW TO PRAY AND RECEIVE ONE!
By Judy O'Halloran

Printed in the United States of America. All rights reserved under International Copyright Law. Contents and/or cover may not be reproduced in whole or in part in any form without the express written consent of the Publisher.

All Scripture used in this book unless otherwise indicated, are taken from the *Holy Bible, New International Version®. Copyright © 1973, 1978, 1984* by the International Bible Society. Used by permission of Zondervan Bible Publishers.

Scripture quotations marked AMP are taken from *The Amplified Bible, Old Testament.* Copyright © 1965, 1987 by the Zondervan Corporation. *The Amplified New Testament,* copyright ©1954, 1958, 1987, by the Lockman Foundation. Used by permission.

Scripture quotations marked KJV are taken from the *King James Version* of the Bible.

Scripture quotations marked NASB are taken from the *New American Standard Bible.* Copyright © 1960, 1962, 1963, 1968, 1971, 1972, 1975, 1977 by the Lockman Foundation. Used by permission.

Scripture quotations marked NKJV are taken from the *New King James Version®.* Copyright © 1982 by Thomas Nelson, Inc. Used by permission. All rights reserved.

Scripture quotations marked NLT are taken from the *Holy Bible, New Living Translation.* Copyright © 1996, 2004, 2007. Used by permission of Tyndale House Publishers, Inc. Carol Stream, Illinois 60188. All rights reserved.

Many names used in this book have been changed.

I Dedicate This Book

*To My Lord and Savior
Jesus Christ*

*To My Three Amazing
Sons*

and

*In Loving Memory of My Husband,
Charlie*

Contents

CHAPTER 1 1
  Do You Have a Burden? 1
CHAPTER 2 10
  You Must Have Faith! 10
CHAPTER 3 16
  Does God Hear You? 16
CHAPTER 4 32
  Who Prayed For You? 32
CHAPTER 5 40
  Pray The Word! 40
CHAPTER 6 48
  Do My Prayers Even Matter? 48
CHAPTER 7 52
  Prayer Depends on Your Life 52
CHAPTER 8 60
  Pray In Secret 60
  Vision Entries from My Sketchbook 70
CHAPTER 9 74
  Following God's Voice 74
CHAPTER 10 82
  Pray With Others! 82
CHAPTER 11 88
  Cry Out! 88
CHAPTER 12 91
  Proclaim Your Life Verse! 91
CHAPTER 13 95
  Persevere! 95
CHAPTER 14 109
  Pray God's Will! 109
CHAPTER 15 114
  Evangelize! 114
CHAPTER 16 119
  Prayerlessness is a Sin! 119

CHAPTER 17 123
    Praying and Expecting Your Miracle 123
CHAPTER 18 130
    Spiritual Warfare and Spiritual Weapons! 130
CONCLUSION 144
REFERENCES 146

HELP! I NEED A **MIRACLE!**
HOW TO PRAY AND RECEIVE ONE!

Do you need a miracle? Do you need God to bring an answer to a prayer you've been praying for years? Are you exhausted, losing hope, or wondering if your prayers even matter at all? That was me when I cried out, "God when are you EVER going to answer one of my prayers?"

I know so many people who need the power of God to show up in their lives and in the lives of their families. They truly need answers to prayers. The great news is that God wants to bring your miracle! Miracles give Him glory, and *YOUR* miracle will glorify God. Unanswered prayer is not because of Him. Why are we not seeing many miracles happening in the Church today? Why are people not getting answers to prayer? Most Christians do not know how to pray according to the Word. I was one of them. I am going to share with you the lessons God taught me concerning biblical prayer, and how I received my miracles. My hope is that by taking you on my journey, you may be blessed with *your* miracle and that God will be glorified!

Chapter 1

DO YOU HAVE A BURDEN?

"...The earnest (heart-felt, continued) prayer of a righteous man makes tremendous power available—dynamic in its working." James 5:16 AMP

ON THE BATTLEFIELD

About twelve years ago, I found myself on a battlefield, fighting in a war that I never expected. I was in battle for the lives of my family! I was attacked with fear, worry, and anxiety. The enemy was after his front line opponent, me! Satan was after the four men in my life, to steal, kill, and destroy them and the great plan and purpose that God had for their lives.

At that time, I knew I was in a battle, but did not know who the real enemy was, his tactics, his schemes, or how to fight. God, in His Word says, "Finally, be strong in the Lord and in His mighty power. Put on the full armor of God so that you can take your stand against the devil's schemes. For our struggle is not against flesh and blood, but against the rulers, against the authorities, against the powers of this dark world and against the spiritual forces of evil in the heavenly realms" (Eph. 6:10-12). I was not prepared for this battle! I had only a vague and incomplete knowledge of the armor I was to put on and no understanding of the devil's schemes specifically designed against me.

However, I turned to, grabbed onto, and knew without a doubt, that God was the one who could help me! "For I am the Lord, your God, who takes hold of your right hand and says to you, Do not fear; I will help you" (Isaiah 41:13). Since that point, God has proved so loving and faithful to lead me, help me, take my right hand, and teach me about His great spiritual weapon, prayer! Derek Prince, author and respected Bible teacher, states it this way, "We who are believers and know how to pray are much more important than most of us have the faintest idea." (*Secrets of a Prayer Warrior,* p.132)

My burden kept me in the battle. You know you have a burden when this desire of your heart won't leave you. Every day it is there. Whenever you talk to God, this is what you keep asking Him for. When you see a number on the television to call for prayer, you get the nudge in your spirit to call, and you do it. When you are asked to write down your prayer requests at a Bible study or church, this is the one or few that you keep asking for. When you are asked to raise your hand in church for a need to be included in the Pastor's prayer, you raise your hand for this burden. When prayer ministers are in front of the church to pray with you after the service, you keep going up for this request. Even if you don't walk to the front, the answer to this prayer is what you long for.

On my first women's retreat from Wheaton Bible Church more than twelve years ago, we were asked to write down our prayer requests. Without hesitation I wrote out my requests because the prayer team for the retreat would faithfully pray over them. The week following the retreat, I received a beautiful card from one of the ladies who prayed for me. I still have this card today and keep it in the center of my dining room table. On the front of the card was a hand-written Bible verse from Lamentations 3:24-26;

I say to myself,
"The Lord is my portion; therefore I will wait for Him."
The Lord is good to those whose hope is in Him,

to the one who seeks Him; it is good to wait patiently, quietly for the salvation of the Lord.

Inside was written:
> Dear Judy, A woman's heart can grow big enough to care for the concerns of each of her family members. Your heart must barely squeeze through your front door! We were privileged to pray along with your heart for the "men" in your life. What a peace to hold onto—knowing that our God is surprised by nothing, confused by nothing, and can work all our mistakes and choices for His great, powerful, loving will. Rest in Jesus—let Him be your burden carrier! You and those you love are prayed for, The Retreat Prayer Team.

I so treasure this verse and card and have reread it many times since receiving it.

During the weekly Bible studies at this church, we would write down our prayer requests. The women at my table would write their requests on one or two lines. They would leave the entire back of the page for me! I was praying for the salvation of my husband and my three teenage sons. I wanted them saved! There were so many things going on at that time and most in the wrong direction. I felt overwhelmed and still remember thinking I was like a plate spinner, trying to keep four plates spinning. I was pretty much a new Christian in a lot of ways, even though I had received Christ twelve years before. I needed to learn how to pray so that my prayers could get answers. There were mountains that needed moving, and these mountains needed miracles. I knew that, "With God all things are possible" (Matt.19:26b), and that is where I put my hope.

It has been a long journey of learning many things

from God about prayer. Through this, I have grown so much in my faith, in His Word, in my plan and purpose, and also in my relationship with Him. Beyond anything, I am so grateful, amazed, and in awe of God. He has worked and blessed me with three MIRACLES since the day I entered the battlefield! Three of the "men" in my life, three of those spinning plates, are on fire for the Lord. My husband is in heaven. Miracle number ONE! He was baptized just 18 days before he died suddenly of a heart attack in the middle of the night at age 56, almost six years ago. God rescued him just in time. My middle son is now a very devoted disciple of Jesus, after being delivered of a very serious drug addiction which lasted seven years. This was over three years ago. Miracle number TWO! And another of my sons was delivered from a dangerous alcohol addiction of also seven years. He just had his one year anniversary of giving his life to the Lord. He was very angry at God and me, but by the grace and mercy of God, is now also a devoted disciple. He, like his brother, is giving his whole life to serving the Lord. Miracle number THREE! These are God's three trophies, shining with His glory! God is so good and so faithful. He really heard my prayers! To God be the glory forever!

Bill Johnson, pastor of Bethel Church in California, says that the absence of miracles actually robs God of the glory He deserves, but when they happen, "Not only do miracles stir the hearts of men to give glory to God, miracles give Him glory on their own." (*When Heaven Invades Earth,* p.125) What God has done in the lives of my husband and sons shows God's power, His purpose, and brings Him glory. God works through prayer and through prayer, He is glorified.

The Secret of Prayer

Burdens are what keep you going in prayer. You do not give up! One thing that the Holy Spirit kept reminding me of when I got so tired of praying and discouraged by not seeing anything change was, "If you aren't praying for them, who is?" Somehow and in some way, He always found a way to get me back up and keep me going. At those "give up" times, He reminded me that I was here "for such a time as this" like Queen Esther assigned to the palace. These men were given to *me* by God, "*for such a time as this*," and it was a job assigned just to me. PRAY for them!

Watchman Nee, a Chinese Christian author and martyr, makes a strong defense for having a burden. He says, " Let us recognize this one thing: burden is the secret of prayer. If a person does not feel within him burden to pray for a particular matter he can hardly succeed in prayer." [My burden was my secret to prayer and God's miracles!] "Without a burden, there is no spiritual value to your work. But with a burden, there is spiritual value." (*Burden and Prayer,* p.1) Carrying a burden to pray for something or someone starts with God. It moves from God's heart to your heart. God wants to bring His will to the earth. It was God's will that my husband and sons come to know Him. God used my prayers to move His will to the earth. This is how Jesus instructed His disciples to pray. In Matthew 6:9-10 we read, "This then is how you should pray, "Our Father in heaven, hallowed be your name, your kingdom come, your will be done, on earth as it is in heaven." God gives burdens to people so they will pray about them. Beni Johnson, who oversees Bethel's intercessors and Prayer House, writes, "My definition for being an *intercessor* is "capturing the heartbeat of Heaven and declaring or praying that into my world. It is true agreement with Heaven." (*The Happy Intercessor,* p.28)

Your Two Enemies

How about you? Are you on the battlefield? Are you praying for a miracle and carrying a heavy burden? Are you willing to devote whatever it takes to see God move and for you to get your answer? It will take time, perhaps years, but that burden you have for someone is worth it, isn't it? This is an important question for you to answer. It will take sacrifice. Prayer is sacrifice of your own time, and it is one of the hardest things for Christians to do. Laziness and prayer cannot exist together. You will get distracted with business, simple chores, crisis situations, relationship issues and attacks from the enemy. Sometimes you will just want to sleep like the disciples did in the Garden of Gethsemane where Jesus asked them to pray with Him three times. Three times He found them sleeping. "Then He returned to His disciples and found them sleeping. 'Could you men not keep watch with me for one hour?' He asked Peter. 'Watch and pray so that you will not fall into temptation. The spirit is willing, but the body is weak" (Matt.26:40-41, NLT). In his book, Roth states it this way, "Getting to prayer is half the battle. Staying there is the other half." (*Prayer Powerpoints,* p.12)

Your body will want to fight the Spirit. It may want to sleep, eat, watch television, call a friend or just complain about something. Know there are two enemies attacking your prayer time—one is Satan and the other is you! God tells us to "...clothe yourselves with the Lord Jesus Christ, and do not think about how to gratify the desires of the sinful nature" (Romans 13:14). He is telling us as Christians, to follow the example of Jesus and do not give sin any opportunity to take over. We must renew our minds with the Word and think on these things to get victory over our flesh. Avoid thinking on thoughts that tempt the flesh.

Prayerlessness is a sin, and not praying for something that God put on your heart to pray for is being disobedient to Him. Intercessory prayer starts in the heart of God. When God gives you a burden, you now have a responsibility to pray. The will of God moves from God's heart to your heart and then through prayer, moves it to God's hand. Putting it in God's hand will bring the miracle. Intercessory prayer requires being sensitive to the Holy Spirit and being obedient and available to God.

Your other enemy, the devil, is smart and cunning and does not want you to pray, because he knows how much your prayers matter to his defeat. A famous quote by Samuel Chadwick, a great preacher on prayer, makes this point, "The one concern of the devil is to keep Christians from praying. He fears nothing from prayerless studies, prayerless work and prayerless religion. He laughs at our toil, mocks at our wisdom, but trembles when we pray." (Roth, Randall, *Prayer Powerpoints*, p.12) When we pray, we are doing spiritual warfare. We are going into enemy territory and claiming what belongs to us as children of the King! John 10:10 describes the war. "The thief comes only to steal, kill, and destroy [us, our family, and our plan and purpose]; I have come that they may have life, and have it to the full."

LET HIM BE YOUR BURDEN CARRIER

One thing that I now realize that I did wrong concerning my burdens was that I carried them *myself*. I did this far too long, and I did not give them up to the One who could work with them. I prayed, brought them to the cross, but did not leave them there. I kept carrying them back home with me. I was carrying them in the flesh and was being crushed under the weight of all the dysfunction around me. But, I knew God told me in His Word that, "His burden was light" (Matt. 11:30). He also said that, "He will not let you be tempted beyond what you could bear" (1 Co. 10:13). I was certainly missing something!

Watchman Nee explains, "If you fail to discharge your burden, it will weigh down heavily on your spirit, and you will feel its weight becoming heavier and heavier as time goes on. . . . If you try to work without a burden, your work will be ineffective. But if you work in accordance with the burden that is upon you, your whole being will be increasingly liberated as you advance." (*Burden and Prayer,* p.3-4)) In Matthew 11:28-30, the Word says, "Come to me, all you who are weary and burdened, and I will give you rest. Take my yoke upon you and learn from me, for I am gentle and humble in heart, and you will find rest for your souls. For my yoke is easy and my burden is light." I was not putting His yoke on me, because if I had, He would have carried the heaviest load, and I would have had what I could manage. I would have had His peace in the situations. I failed to rest in His Word.

With each miracle, however, my faith and trust grew. When I saw what God did in my husband's life, I saw His power and His faithfulness. I was gradually learning how to trust God. I gradually began to do it God's way and not get crushed by carrying my own burden. I prayed, I carried it to the cross, and I left it there with the One who could take care of it. Now, I did not do this perfectly, I still wobbled some, but I was making progress and learning to release the burden. Perry Stone helps explain this when he writes, "Never quit praying as long as your spirit remains restless. Only when the burden lifts should you arise from your prayer position." (*Opening The Gates of Heaven,* p.142) As my faith grew, my burden would lift faster, and I would feel peace about it. When God puts a burden on your heart, you must learn to recognize it, pray about it, and then release it. He is so faithful. My faith was growing and I was honoring God by trusting Him more and more. I learned that He can't work with something I hold onto. Only when it is released to Him, can He release a blessing back.

I also learned that meditating on specific Scriptures is a great way to release the burden. The Word says, "Casting all your care upon Him because He cares for you" (1Pe 5:7, NKJ). We are not to be anxious about the burden we are carrying when we pray for someone. We are to be at peace about it, knowing that God hears us: and be confident that God will perfect it. A great verse that gives me so much peace and helps me release a burden is Psalm 138:8, "The Lord will perfect that which concerns me" (NKJ). It covers every situation, and I use this verse often!

Jesus, Himself, shows us what to do. He is our example. In Isaiah 53:4 we read about Jesus being a burden bearer. It says, "Yet it was our weaknesses He carried, and it was our sorrows that weighed Him down" (NLT). Jesus was without sin and carried our burdens. Also we read in Isaiah 53:12b how Jesus interceded for us sinners. "He bore the sins of many and interceded for rebels" (NLT). We use Jesus as our example to follow in praying for those who are lost. He had such a burden for His lost, and He did something about it. One thing He did was pray! Then He took it to the cross. When do you stop praying? When God takes the burden away. My burdens did not go away until I saw the answers—God's will on earth, His Miracles!

*****

My burden was for my family. I wanted so much for them to be saved and able to go to heaven; so did God! Their lives showed that they couldn't care less. This took me on a journey to learn more about prayer. I was praying and crying out to God, but mountains did not seem to move. This motivated me to learn *more* and *more* about prayer! I so wanted to see God move! I will share with you and encourage you that prayer works. It is how God works. If you are not seeing God answering your prayers, then learn more about God and what He says about prayer. There is so much to learn from the Word about this most important ministry. Someone you love needs your prayers. Their life is depending on them!

Chapter 2

YOU MUST HAVE FAITH!

"Without faith, it is impossible to please God." Hebrews 11:6

One thing that is needed to get your miracle is to pray with faith. Without faith there is no power, no substance, and no reward. We **must** have faith in the **One** to whom we are praying to for our miracle. Hebrews 11:6 in the NIV reads, *"And without faith it is impossible to please God,"* because *anyone who comes to him must believe he exists and that he rewards those who earnestly seek him.* In the NLT it reads, *"And it is impossible to please God without faith. Anyone who wants to come to him must believe that God exists and that he rewards those who sincerely seek him."* The King James Bible reads, *"But without faith it is impossible to please him: for he that cometh to God must believe that he is, and that he is a rewarder of them that diligently seek him."* God will reward the one who has the faith to earnestly, sincerely, and diligently seek and search for Him! He is so pleased when we put ALL our faith in Him, that we come to Him for our help and answer. He is the answer!

My Spiritual Intervention

I cannot remember who told me this, but it had to be one of the three people that were present. One day, my mother, my husband and my son, Colin, had a meeting at my mother's house, and it was to talk about *me*! They felt I needed a spiritual intervention. They were concerned with my obsession to the things of God and the way I was pressing into the Lord, the Word, and Christian friends. There was something that they did not recognize about me, and they actually felt I needed help! I knew I needed Him, and I was seeking Him with all my heart. When my world was falling apart all around me, I knew who had my answer! Actually, I really like this story, to think that they actually were serious about this!

At that time, my husband and I were involved in marriage counseling, and Charlie asked me to see an additional counselor because he felt I really needed to be "evaluated"! He knew there was something different going on with me and could not figure it out. I seemed like an "alien, stranger, or foreigner" to him. God was changing me! I remember clearly a time when The Holy Spirit definitely spoke to me about my relationship with Him. A few years prior to my "evaluation session", I was very convicted listening to a Sunday sermon at my church. It was about Matt. 7:21-23 which says, "Not everyone who says to me, 'Lord, Lord', will enter the kingdom of heaven, but only the one who does the will of my Father who is in heaven. Many will say to me on that day, 'Lord, Lord, did we not prophesy in your name, and in your name drive out demons and perform many miracles?' Then I will tell them plainly, 'I never knew you. Away from me, you evildoers!' " I was giving this some serious thought! God was speaking to me!

Two things concerned me about my Christian walk. One was that I had daily devotion time and read the Bible, but I did it only as something I had to do. It was something I checked off as done, and I did not look that forward to it. The second thing was that I could not quite understand how people could give up their time to serve at church or elsewhere. Those two things I questioned about myself. Then that same week, I was listening to the Moody Radio Station as I was driving in my car and that same verse came up! Now God totally had my attention. I imagined myself getting up to heaven, facing God, and Him saying that He never really knew me! "Depart!" Right then in the car, I remember calling out to God, "Lord, if I do not have the kind of faith that gets me into heaven, please do something!" He did something! I became an alien, a very serious one! I became one whose husband thinks she needs to be stopped through a spiritual intervention! Charlie said that, "I was so heavenly minded, I was no earthly good." What was interesting about this comment was that when I heard John Piper speak at Wheaton College a few years later, he said that we must be so heavenly minded so we *can* do earthly good! I had to smile at that! God did a spiritual intervention, and I now knew that He *knew* me. Praise God!

Being Different

Acts 16:31 says to, "Believe on the Lord Jesus Christ, and you will be saved, you and your household" (NKJ). Believe on the Lord does not mean to believe about the Lord. Believe on the Lord means to believe in such a way that your life changes. He becomes your Lord. Your household has to believe in Jesus just as you do to be saved, but if one person in a household has a saving faith, God is in the majority. The whole family can come to a saving faith if you have the kind of faith that diligently searches and seeks Him. He promises to reward this kind of faith.

Does your family see you pressing into Jesus? Are you different from the world? The Bible says that we are aliens here. 1 Peter 2:11 reads, "Dear friends, I urge you, as aliens and strangers in the world, to abstain from sinful desires which war against your soul." In John 17: 14 & 16, Jesus says about believers, "I have given them your word and the world has hated them, for they are not of the world any more than I am of the world. They are not of the world, even as I am not of it." That means that we should not blend in or look like those that are of the world.

Bill Johnson, pastor and author, writes that one thought we need to comprehend in order to understand prayer is "as disciples we are both citizens and ambassadors of another world. This world is our assignment, but not our home. Our purpose is eternal. The resources needed to complete the assignment are unlimited." With faith in God, we have everything available to us. We just need to know how to tap into it through prayer. "...with faith...We have all the power of heaven behind us. But, it is our faith that connects what is available to the circumstances at hand. Faith takes what is available and makes it actual." (*When Heaven Invades Earth*, p.55, 58) Our actual is our miracle!

The kind of faith that pleases God is the "earnestly seeking Him" kind. On a scale of one to ten, rate yourself in the area of diligently, sincerely, and earnestly seeking Him. This might be an indication of how close or far away you are to your miracle. If you feel like you are average on that scale, you may want to cry out to the Lord, "Lord, please, do something!"

Just to confirm that God heard my prayer and "did something," I would say that in this area, He did, "abundantly beyond all that I could ask or think" (Eph.3: 20, NASB). The two areas that God shed light on in my resistant heart were my attitude toward reading His Word and serving. These He changed radically! I am now addicted to His Word and in total pursuit of serving Him through His number one desire — changing me! The more He changes me, the more I am able to reach others for His Kingdom.

THE MINISTRY OF CHANGE

Our number one ministry is ourselves — to change and become more and more like Christ. This is called sanctification. I did not know about this for almost half of my

Christian life. I had a lot of catching up to do! How comforting to know that this is His job description, not mine. He will do it! He promises! "Being confident of this, that He who began a good work in you will carry it on to completion until the day of Christ Jesus" (Phil. 1:6). When I meet Him face-to-face, He will have completed His work in me. I will be just like Him. Until that day, however, the sanctification process is hard work!

Sometimes sanctification is excruciatingly painful. Going through difficult trials has a way of forcing you to your knees and crying out to Him. This is God's best classroom, the "on our knees, arms raised, all ears, only two in the room" class! Real learning takes place here. We pay attention to every word, written or whispered! I know this classroom very well. The atmosphere is one of love, compassion, and acceptance. It is a place where I hear my Father say: "So glad you are here.", "Do not worry," "I am catching every tear.", "Be still.", and "I will help you!" It is one in which I have found strength to go on. It is here where I have surrendered my will for His will and put my way on the altar. This is when miracles have a way of showing up! When I was seeking Him with all my heart, He had my attention, and the rest of the world had to be pushed aside, which made room for Him to bring the miracles!

God was working on changing me in the area of prayer. Through my trials, He taught me much about prayer. I learned that God is *waiting* to answer my prayer, and His *desire* is to answer my prayer. He wants the answer more than I do because He wants His will done on the earth. Andrew Murray writes, "The Father waits to hear every prayer of faith...God intends prayer to have an answer, no one has yet fully conceived what God will do for the child who believes that his prayer will be heard. *God hears prayer."* (*With Christ in the School of Prayer,* p.7-8)

Jesus would not have taught His disciples to pray, "Thy Kingdom Come. Thy will be done, in earth as it is in heaven" ((Matt. 6:10, KJV), if it did not matter. Jesus was always in communication with the Father! He modeled prayer. Your prayers matter, and the faith behind those prayers matters. I believe that there is no other part of Christ's life that is more important for us as followers to imitate and learn more about than prayer. Jesus was always in the presence of His Father, continually in communication with Him as an intercessor for us. We are to do this, we can do this, and we must do this for others! Andrew Murray says our lives need to become lives that, "continuously pray for men." (*With Christ in the School of Prayer,* p.7) For most of us, including me, this change is quite a challenge, but with God, it is possible!

*****

If you have the kind of faith that pleases God, then you have a life that has evidence of change! You too have had a spiritual intervention! Praise God! Now *earnestly* seek Him and get your promised reward. Get ready for your miracle.

Chapter 3

DOES GOD HEAR YOU?

"For the eyes of the Lord are on the righteous, and his ears are open to their prayers." 1Peter 3:12a (NKJV)

Don't waste time praying if you have a wall up between you and God! He can't hear you! The only prayer He can hear from your side of the wall is a prayer of repentance! In the verse above, we read that God is open to the prayers of the righteous. Righteous does not mean our righteousness, but the righteousness of Christ. Romans 3:23 says that, "We all have sinned and fall short of the glory of God." We are to "Seek first the kingdom of God and His righteousness, and all these things shall be added onto you" (Matt. 6:33, KJV). God tells us where to find this righteousness in Romans 3:22, "This righteousness from God comes through faith in Jesus Christ to all who believe." This is the first and most important step to praying for your miracle, knowing that the first miracle God wants to work is in YOU!

Bill Johnson, in his book about miracles, writes, "Not one of us understood salvation until we were saved. It was the miracle — an experience — which gave us understanding." (*When Heaven Invades Earth,* 130) Many people think that they are saved; that they are Christians, but have never had that "experience" when God reaches down into a repentant heart that turns to Him and gives new birth to his spirit. This is not a change with an increase of knowledge about Jesus. Satan agrees who Jesus is; knows all about Him. This is a total change of DNA, a life changing experience, and God's greatest miracle! God describes it like this, ". . .If anyone is in Christ, he is a new creation, the old has gone, the new has come!" (2Cor.5:17).

My First Miracle – Charlie

You can be deceived like my husband was for so many years. My husband, Charlie, agreed with the gospel message, that Jesus was the only way to God. He went to church, attended some Bible studies, read the Word, and even evangelized on occasion, explaining salvation to people. When our sons were young, we both helped at Awana Club, listening to children recite Scripture. However, during the last few years of Charlie's life, I questioned if his faith was real. His focus became that of becoming rich to the point that it became an idol. He questioned my faith and then our marriage. People he started to spend time with were not those who were holding him accountable, but just agreeing with him. He seemed to be going down a very slippery slope.

I remember one day, crying outside in my driveway, when my wonderful Christian neighbor, Alice, came over. I was in tears about my husband. I remember her asking me this question, "Is he a Christian?" I answered, " I am not sure anymore." I started to question, what does it take to be saved? John 3:16 says, "...that whosoever believes in Him, shall not perish, but have eternal life." I learned that this "believe" means not believe "about", but believe "in." It means trust in, rely on, follow, give your life to, and agree with Him. You cannot keep your life and give it up at the same time. You cannot face and walk in your own direction and also face God and follow Him at the same time. I saw confusion in my husband and felt darkness taking over our home. But the Spirit of God was hovering over this man, and God was putting His plan in place.

God went to work rearranging things in my husband's life. Out of nowhere with us not having one previous thought about it, He opened a door for us to move to Florida and for Charlie to expand his appraisal business there. Our original plan at that time was to spend six months in Florida and six in Chicago after my youngest son completed his last two years of high school. Shane was transferring to a Christian High School in Fort Myers, Florida, and I hoped that this would help one member of our family survive!

While my husband was commuting back and forth between Chicago and Fort Myers, maintaining the Chicago business, his life went way out of control. Looking back on this time, I see how God was able to use it for good. Charlie was spending a lot of money on the maintenance of his older Mercedes and was considering selling it and leasing a car. I saw an advertisement on television about leasing and saw how you could lease a good car for a reasonable amount — a good family type car. We talked about it, and he looked further into it. That led to him leasing a black, fast, GTO, for not a reasonable amount! My family up in Chicago was having a family get-together, and my mother told me she heard this, "vroom, vroom", quite loud noise outside. It was Charlie in his new car. He gave many of his nephews rides in it that day. My son Shane told me this story later, how Dad let him drive it, and he said it got up to 150 miles an hour!!

One person Charlie spent a great deal of time with while in Chicago was a young man in his late 20's who also wanted to get rich! They had similar goals; making money. This person smoked and so Charlie started smoking cigarettes. Later I found out his addiction got up to four packs a day. Now that could be an exaggeration, but from what I sensed, this could be true. He came down to Fort Myers for one of his weekend visits and his skin just reeked of smoke. I said, "Charlie, are you smoking?!!" I could not believe it. I had never seen him smoke, ever! I knew that he did smoke before I met him. Actually I think the story goes that he started in Junior High. Charlie and I met when we were both doing a health and nutrition business, and he had stopped smoking because of this. It had been over twenty years. This was a pivotal point in Charlie's miracle.

I could see that this Chicago, Florida idea was not working for the better. That week, I confided in a strong Christian man, a father of a player on my son's baseball team, about my husband's smoking. He wisely said, "It is not good for a husband and wife to be separated like you are." The Holy Spirit convicted me. It now was not about Shane going to a Christian School anymore. It was about Charlie. I talked with God and told Him that I wanted to obey Him by not putting my son ahead of my husband. I was not thinking what would be good for Shane anymore. If He wanted me to, I would move back to Chicago. That Sunday at church God clearly spoke to me. He spoke loud and clear. I was at church by myself; I remember the place I was sitting. I was looking at the pastor, knowing that Charlie really loved this church and pastor. I just said to God, "Where do you want me?" God said to me, "I want Charlie down here!" When you know that you really heard from God, you have clear direction. It was very clear!

On the way home from church, I called Charlie and said that he should move down full-time to Fort Myers. He was ready to hear this. In Wheaton, a suburb of Chicago, we had signed a one year lease with an option to lease a second year. He notified the owner that we were not going to lease the second year. Three months later, Charlie arrived in Florida. However, those last three months in Chicago magnified Charlie's need for God to rescue him. Later I heard how my husband was smoking marijuana with one of my sons who was still in Chicago. Besides the cigarette smoke, there was yet another kind. Oddly enough or should I say miraculously enough, while he smoked in this apartment, he continuously watched a DVD of a Christian Concert filmed in Colorado. Charlie loved watching these passionate worshipers and the Holy Spirit was drawing him.

Charlie packed up his GTO and started driving south. On his drive down to Florida, he stopped in Georgia to see some friends who actually grew marijuana on their property! Charlie was on the fence and needed to make a choice. How had he gotten so far away from the day almost twenty-two years before when we both walked forward to accept Christ at a Christian Church in Boca Raton, Florida called Bible Town? We also attended our first Christian concert at James Kennedy's church in Fort Lauderdale. The singer was David Meeks.

One of the first things Charlie said after moving down to Florida was, "I want to evangelize." I thought that was a positive mission statement, but I said to myself, "First God is going to evangelize you." And that is exactly what God did! Over the next nine months, God worked a miracle in my husband. It is interesting how this number is nine months, the same time it takes for natural birth. The one book I was reading at that time was about prayer, and it had a chapter titled, "Supernatural Childbirth." This was exactly what I needed to study; what prayers birth Christians? I learned about travailing prayer and that my prayers for my husband mattered.

The Holy Spirit is the one who gives new birth to a man's spirit. God tells us that "Unless one is born again, he cannot see the Kingdom of God" (John 3:3, NASB). I read about travailing prayer or birthing prayer. In his book, Dutch Sheets explains that, "There is an aspect of prayer that births things in the Spirit. We are "birthers" for God. The Holy Spirit wants to "bring forth" through us. ...We are the womb of God upon the earth. We are not the source of life, but we are the carriers of the source of life. We do not generate life, but we release, through prayer, Him who does." (*Intercessory Prayer*, p.116) We are to intercede for others through travailing prayer. The Holy Spirit will work with us as we read in Romans 8: 26-27, "Likewise the Spirit also helps in our weaknesses. For we do not know what we should pray for as we ought. But the Spirit Himself makes intercession for us with groanings which cannot be uttered. Now he who searches the heart knows what the mind of the Spirit is, because He makes intercession for the saints according to the will of God" (NKJV). Also we read in Isaiah 66:8 about this birthing prayer of travail, "as soon as Zion travailed she brought forth her children" (KJV). Paul prayed for new believers this way, "My little children, of whom I travail in birth again until Christ be formed in you" (Gal. 4:19, KJV). Travailing prayer combines with the power of the Holy Spirit to bring about God's will in the life of a person. It brings about a new life in the spirit. In James we read this prayer as fervent prayer. "The fervent prayer of a righteous man, availeth much" (James 5:16, KJV).

I started praying travailing, fervent prayers for my husband. At night, while Charlie was sleeping, I would ask the Holy Spirit to hover over my husband's spirit and give it life! As the Holy Spirit hovered over the confusion as we read in Genesis—when He hovered over the waters and then birthed order to the earth—I asked the Holy Spirit to bring order into Charlie's life. Dutch Sheets describes, "He [the Holy Spirit] wants to go forth and hover around individuals, releasing His awesome power to convict, break bondages, bring revelation and draw them to Himself in order to cause the new birth or new creation in them. Yes, the Holy Spirit wants to birth through us." He defines travailing intercession like this: "A form of intercession that releases the creative power or energy of the Holy Spirit into a situation to produce, create or give birth to something." (*Intercessory Prayer,* p.123, 128)

Something started happening. Charlie started changing. The Holy Spirit was convicting him. Sometime between my birthday which was in January and April 22, which was the day Charlie was baptized, one of our pastors told me, "Something got hold of Charlie. Charlie was changing." This gave me hope, because I was not seeing it yet!

I still remember the events of my birthday that year. As the day went on, I could sense that Charlie was not going to buy me anything or plan anything to celebrate my birthday. Then at the last minute, he went out and bought me a few presents. He still had a very hardened heart. The gifts had nothing to do with God or anything Christian, just some simple items relating to our new home in Fort Myers. This was significant because I knew the point he was trying to make. I knew my husband and what he was thinking. He was still not letting God in and wanted me to know that. I kept praying! I travailed in prayer for him. God kept working.

We kept going to church, but I knew that Charlie needed more than church; he needed to be around other Christian men. I asked a lady I knew at church which Sunday school class she would recommend. She had a copy of the book, *Driven by Eternity,* tucked under her arm, pulled it out and said, "This one." I was not sure if Charlie would go to a class followed by a church service on Sunday morning. This meant 9:30 and then 11:15. I prayed to God that He would make this happen. He did! It was in this Sunday school class, taught by Pastor Grant, that Charlie studied this book by John Bevere. When we joined, the class was already on chapter 9, and in preparation for the next week, we were to read chapter 10. Charlie started at the beginning and caught up by the next class. I started on Chapter 10. My husband was a more devoted student than me, and he was now seeking! The truths in this book and getting to see the lifestyles of the Christian men in our class, were all playing a part in God's miracle.

Our middle son, Brian, had now moved down to Florida with us. I asked Pastor Grant if he would meet with my son, Brian, who was struggling with many things including a drug addiction. My husband, Charlie, brought Brian to this meeting. Pastor Grant said that within five minutes, he could tell that this meeting was more for Charlie than for Brian. Charlie was seeking.

Charlie started stopping by the church to talk with Pastor Grant. He kept reading and studying the book from our class and attending Sunday services which he loved. He even started serving at the coffee bar in the back of the church. In March, Charlie attended a five day Christian leadership conference held at Southeastern University in Florida, with my oldest son, Colin, who was still living in the Chicago area. Some of the guest speakers were Tony Dungy, Tommy Barnett, Tony Evans and John Maxwell. Charlie and I were both interested in going to this, but we thought it would be a great event for Colin to go to instead of me. Charlie asked him if he wanted to go and he agreed! This proved to be a very valuable and significant time for both of them. One of the reasons was that Colin saw his Dad totally changed. The passion that Colin saw his father have for business and money was now a passion for hearing about God. Charlie did not want to miss a minute of the conference, took many notes, and purchased the DVD's of the conference for both my son and himself. God was working. Charlie was changing. I kept praying!

On April 22, at a Wednesday night church service, Charlie was baptized. It was the night that Teen Challenge was there. This was interesting because two years before, Teen Challenge was the one place I wanted my son Brian to go to for help, but Charlie did not agree. He said they would shove religion at him. Teen Challenge is an international Christian drug and alcohol rehabilitation program. However, this night, he would have agreed that it would have been the best thing to do. Not only was Charlie baptized, but he also left an amazing legacy that night by the words he spoke. He was leaving an inheritance for his children and his children's, children. It was not about money, it was about spiritual wealth. The pastor who was doing the baptism asked if Charlie had any words to say. This is what my husband struggled to say as he held back tears: "I spent probably half my life abusing drugs and alcohol. Had tremendous anger. And I realized here recently, that even though I stopped doing a lot of those things, I was still selfish. I am very thankful to this church. I would like to apologize to my wife, my family, and to God... and I am just glad that Jesus is going to acknowledge me before His Father." Pastor said, "The power of the cross, transforming another human being." Then Charlie was placed under the water and came up with a smile and an "alright!"

On the paper that our church had people fill out before they get baptized, Charlie wrote:

Describe your life: A train wreck.

What brings you here today? It has been a long road very slowly leaving things of this world behind. Mostly I was lukewarm and deceived most of this time. This church these past 8 months has taught me much.

On Friday, May 4th, near noon, I called Charlie on his cell phone, and he said he was meeting Pastor Grant for lunch. What a blessing to hear this. Later I was let in on their conversation. Charlie said, "Pastor, I finally got it. All this stuff that I have been accumulating, it doesn't matter. It is all going to be burnt up. I have been attending church for 20 years, and I just now realize that I am a lukewarm Christian. I am not hot. I am going to die, and God is going to spit me out of His mouth. He is talking to me. I don't care anymore about stuff. I can live in a double-wide." Charlie was referring to a book we were studying in our Sunday school class and the verse we find in Revelation 3:16, "So, because you are lukewarm—neither hot nor cold—I am about to spit you out of my mouth."

The Holy Spirit convicted Charlie through this book and verse. He realized that he had been indifferent to the things of God and to what Jesus did on the cross for him. He had been sitting in church all these years, being self-sufficient and drawn to things of this world. Charlie grew farther and farther away from God, until he came to his senses. The enemy's scheme for my husband's soul worked far too long, but God, in His time and His way, drew Charlie near. My husband finally knew what was real, a right relationship with God the Father through Jesus. What Charlie was searching for all his life, he finally found. He found God! The Bible says that, "You will seek me and find me, when you seek me with all of your heart" (Jeremiah 29:13).

God arranged things so that Charlie would find Him. He opened the door to moving to Florida, to the church, to the Bible Study, to Christian men, to a book, to a Pastor and to Him. Wow! God, You are amazing! Charlie had the "experience" of a changed heart. He no longer had head knowledge; he had a spirit that was born again through the power of the Blood of Jesus. Eighteen days after his baptism, Charlie died suddenly of a heart attack in the middle of the night. Jesus took him home and presented him to his Father in heaven.

*****

On Charlie's gravestone, I had engraved:

> CHARLES R. O'HALLORAN
> BORN JULY 3, 1950
> BAPTIZED APR. 22, 2007
> IN GOD'S KINGDOM MAY 10, 2007
>
> I TELL YOU THE TRUTH, NO ONE CAN SEE THE KINGDOM OF GOD UNLESS HE IS BORN AGAIN. JOHN 3:3

Although this was definitely a shock and not what I planned for, I also saw it as a miracle! I felt like I was in the middle of a Bible story. I was in the middle of God's story for me and for Charlie. I prayed, God saved, and Charlie was welcomed into heaven wrapped in the Father's arms. Losing my husband was very difficult and sad, but knowing what God had done and knowing where Charlie was, gave me peace.

Do You Know God?

Charlie was on the fence for over twenty years. He did not realize who owned the fence. What side of the fence are you on? Here is a great little story to think about.

> There is a story about the day of reckoning when Jesus and the devil came to a meadow to take their followers to their eternal destination. There was a fence in the meadow, and one man thought he could skip the judgment by sitting on the fence. After everyone had departed, the devil came back and said, "Oh there you are, come with me?" "Why, I'm on the fence." And the devil said, "I own the fence."

Duane Matz tells this story and explains that this fence is a fence of indifference and indecision to what Jesus did on the cross and it is not a good place to sit. ("The Daily Du-Votional", http://todayslivingword.blogspot.com/2011/10/devil-owns-fence.html.)

To be able to pray to God and for Him to hear you, you must know Him. In order to abide in Christ and in His presence, He must know you. There must be a relationship. In Matthew 7:23 it is very clear that God warns us strongly about not being a hypocrite. He says, "Then I will tell them plainly, 'I never knew you, away from me you evil doers.'" God has relationship with followers only.

Billy Graham's grandson, Tullian Tchividjian, pastor and author, explains that, "It is absolutely true: we can enter into an eternal relationship with God only through faith in Jesus Christ and what He accomplished on the cross. God rescues us; we don't rescue ourselves." He then talks about how the Bible mentions two different kinds of faith; one is dead faith and the other living faith. Living faith we read about in 1John 2:3, "By this we know that we have come to know him, if we keep his commandments" (NASB). Dead faith we read about in James 2:17, "Thus also faith by itself, if it does not have works, is dead" (NKJV). "Dead faith is faith in God that doesn't lead to a changed life. People with dead faith profess to believe in Christ, but their lives haven't changed." "Living faith, on the other hand, is faith in God that leads to genuine life changes. People with living faith express it in and through their thoughts, affections, and actions. It completely changes how someone lives and what he loves." (*Do I Know God? 75, 78, 77*)

At a Kay Arthur conference in Orlando, Florida, the one thing she said that I remember to this day is this: "If you are born again, your life has changed. If your life has not changed, you need to be born again." Giving your life to Jesus, making Him the Lord of your life, results in a changed life. How do we know if we know God? Our life has changed.

To receive a miracle from God, you need to know Him. Author Linda Shepherd explains how this is the first requirement in being able to pray for and receive your miracle. Knowing about Jesus and His fame is not the same as knowing Him as your Savior and close friend.

> Sadly, a person who has head knowledge about God's fame, but has never taken the time to connect with him through prayer or pursue forgiveness of sins through Jesus does not have a relationship with him. So how can we connect with God? The good news is that God, unlike most celebrities, will answer us when we call. And if we want a relationship with God, we must call upon him. Otherwise, he may tell you on the day you meet him on the other side of eternity, "I never knew you. Away from

me" (Matt. 7:23). (*When You Need a Miracle,* 19)

This does not have to be you! Remember the one prayer that God hears from the other side of the wall is the prayer of repentance. This could be the first miracle you need to see in your life. The miracle prayer you need for yourself. The one that saves you for all eternity! The following is part of a wonderful prayer given out by the River Church in Tampa, Florida, which has been used by hundreds of people to pray with thousands all over the world!

> Has anyone ever told you that God loves you and that He has a wonderful plan for your life? If you were to die this very second, do you know for sure, beyond a shadow of a doubt, that you would go to Heaven? Let me quickly share with you what the Holy Bible reads. It reads, "for all have sinned and come short of the glory of God" (Rom. 3:23, KJV) and "for the wages of sin is death, but the gift of God is eternal life through Jesus Christ our Lord" (Rom. 6:23, KJV). The Bible also reads, "For whosoever shall call upon the name of the Lord shall be saved" (Rom. 10:13, KJV). And you are a "whosoever!" ... If you would like to receive the gift that God has for you, say this prayer with your heart and lips out loud.
> Dear Lord Jesus, come into my heart. Forgive me of my sin. Wash me and cleanse me. Set me free. Jesus, thank You that You died for me. I believe that You are risen from the dead and that You're coming back again for me. Fill me with the Holy Spirit. Give me a passion for the lost, and a hunger for the things of God and a holy boldness to preach the gospel of Jesus

Christ. I'm saved; I'm born again, I'm forgiven and I'm on my way to Heaven because I have Jesus in my heart... (River Church at Tampa Bay, www.revival.com/river).

The River Church evangelism team came to our town to do a one week long, soul winning evangelism training. We used this script and went to houses, shopping malls, parking lots, schools, and nursing homes. My favorite testimony was from a young girl around 20 years old, who went out evangelizing for the very first time. She went with a small group to find groups of people, and they visited high schools. This girl approached the football coach and asked if she could pray with his team. They were in the middle of football practice! She said the entire football team got down on their knees and prayed this prayer and gave their lives to Jesus! Then they went to the cheerleading squad, and did the same! Wow! Amen!

One of my most special memories was having the opportunity to pray this prayer with a man in the nursing home, who was not very old, possibly in his forties. He was very sick and could barely talk because he had a tracheostomy. I got close enough to his face so I could see his eyes and so he could hear me. He struggled to talk, but managed to softly say this prayer out loud as best he could. I knew it was a heartfelt prayer by reading his eyes and seeing the tears roll down the sides of his face. After we finished, he had a slight smile and his eyes glowed of freedom. I knew God had worked a miracle!

Linda Shepherd also includes a prayer to accept Jesus as Lord and Savior in her book. Making Jesus the Lord of your life is the very first thing that must be done to be able to have a relationship with God. This was the whole meaning, the whole purpose of why Jesus had to go to the cross. Sin separates us from God. But, by receiving the free gift of what Jesus did on the cross, you are seen as the righteousness of Christ, just as if you have never sinned. You are put in right standing with God, and you are now His child who He receives with open arms. Shepherd says, "Rejoice that you know you have a relationship with God. But your job isn't done. Now it's time to grow in that relationship. The more you invite God into your life, the more you'll learn how to rest in his abiding presence and the more miracles you'll see." (*When You Need a Miracle,* p.20)

How do you grow in this new relationship with God? Start by reading the Bible. Once I heard a pastor say that he tells new believers to read John 3, *three* times. Besides daily reading of the Word, have fellowship with other believers by finding a good church that teaches and obeys the Bible. God wants His children to be part of a local body of believers. Find time to spend alone with the Lord each day and grow in the awareness of His presence. "My sheep listen to my voice; I know them, and they follow me" (John 10:27-28).

Now, as believers we have access to God. Through the free gift of salvation, we are restored to a relationship with our heavenly Father because the sin that separated us has been washed away with Jesus' blood. We are cleansed from all unrighteousness, and because of this, Hebrews 4:16 tells us to come to God the Father with confidence. "Let us then approach the throne of grace with confidence so that we may receive mercy and find grace to help us in our time of need." Through prayer, we are able to come to the throne of God knowing that He will have mercy on us and help us. Without this relationship, there is no access to God, and He does not hear your prayers. So, do it right now! Ask Jesus into your life. Then, meet God Your Father in the throne room! He can't wait to see you! Oh, how He has been waiting for you!

Chapter 4

WHO PRAYED FOR YOU?

"As For me, God forbid that I should sin against the Lord in ceasing to pray for You." 1 Samuel 12:23 (KJV)

My youngest son won a baseball scholarship to Covenant College in Chattanooga, Tennessee. This was an amazingly beautiful Christian school at the top of Lookout Mountain. It was a great school but a very difficult school to visit, traveling from Fort Myers, Florida. However, I did find a way to get to one of his fall practices. The one thing I remembered most about that trip was a question that the father of one of the players asked me. Since we were at a very conservative Christian College, he assumed I was a believer in Jesus Christ, so he asked me, "So, who prayed for you?" What he was asking was, who was it that prayed for you so that you could come to know Christ. I never thought about it that seriously until then. He said it in such a "without a doubt, someone prayed you in" way, that I never forgot it.

JOY!

I am thankful to my sister Joy who prayed for me. She became a Christian about three years before I did, and she invited me to a Christian church where I heard the gospel message for the first time. What is interesting about this is that she said she came to know the Lord through reading the Bible. The Bible she read was the one I gave her for her wedding. I was not a Christian at the time, nor was she, and neither of us ever read the Bible. I just thought it was a good gift to give her and her husband for a wedding present with their name engraved on it. What an amazingly great gift that was! I believe it was the best gift I ever gave anyone!

Recently she told me the story of how she came to read the Bible. Early in their marriage, Joy and her husband Nick moved to Pennsylvania away from their families who lived in the Chicago area. They had their first child, and my sister was at home alone much of the time because her husband traveled for business. For something to do, she decided to read. Because she did not grow up as a reader, she said she did not own any books except for the Bible I gave her. She decided to read it! After reading from the Bible, she knew that what she read was not the same as the theology she grew up with. Both could not be true. One had to be false. When they moved back to Chicago, her sister-in-law who was a Christian, verbalized the gospel message to her and Joy said, "It just clicked!" The Holy Spirit clicked! That is when she got revelation of the truth of the Bible and was born again, receiving Jesus as her Lord and Savior.

Joy's husband also came to know the Lord after they started attending a Christian church. Willow Creek was at that time meeting in a theater. Nick said that he thought Joy had talked to Pastor Bill Hybels before the services because he felt the pastor was speaking directly to him. After Nick made Jesus his Lord, they began praying together for their families to also come to a saving faith in Christ. I am so thankful those prayers included me!

Their prayers got *me* to this church where I heard exactly what I needed to hear. I will never forget the sermon that day. It was about how God is not only a loving God, but also a *just* God. I thought of God as only loving, and that He sent only *really bad* sinners to hell. God doesn't send people to hell, sin does! I learned a **just** and **holy** God must judge *all* sin and sin must be punished. "For the wages of sin is death

[hell], but the gift of God is eternal life through Christ Jesus our Lord" (Rom. 6:23). A *holy* God cannot allow sin into heaven! My *loving* God provided the way! Jesus took my place and died on the cross for my sin. There was *nothing* I could do about my sin. I could not do penance, be good enough, do good works or obey rules. I was presented the truth, and by the grace of God I believed it and *received* it by faith! My life changed that day for all eternity!! I went from my wrong believing to believing the truth that set me free! On my refrigerator I have a magnet that reads, "God grades on the cross, not the curve!" This describes how my beliefs changed that day, and I made the decision to make Jesus *my* Lord and Savior. The Holy Spirit revealed truth to my spirit, and I was "born again!" (John 3:3). Prayers for *me* were answered! I love that story!

I am sure my sister's prayers added to my mother's. When I was in college, my mother became a Christian. She was invited to a home Bible study of one of her friends. She told me she remembers reading "The Four Spiritual Laws" tract. She also started attending a Bible-believing Christian church, and she is still attending there today some forty years later. I know that she started praying for her nine children and her husband to come to know Jesus as Lord and Savior. I am thankful for my mother's prayers for me. After I became a believer, I added my prayers to my mother's prayers for my father, and he is now in heaven!

Pastor Solomon

One Saturday afternoon, I received a call from my sister-in-law, Mary Lu. She was all excited about a young pastor she sat next to on her 14 hour plane trip back from India. She was in India for the wedding of her son-in-law's brother. Pastor Solomon works for Hope for Today Ministries where he is the administrative coordinator. They have planted 78 churches in India, and he oversees 30 pastors and 7 slum schools which are Christian schools offered at no cost to children from the slums. Mary Lu told me that the first church Pastor Solomon was going to speak at was in Fort Myers, Florida! She so wanted me to meet him.

I was able to locate where he would be speaking the next day and was blessed to hear his testimony. He came to a saving faith at the age of 17 although he was raised in a Hindu home. He said that when he was in seventh grade, he would go to Sunday school with some Christian friends who lived in his neighborhood. At Sunday school they were rewarded for memorizing Scripture. He went only for the fun and prizes, but actually memorized more than 100 Scriptures. His father who was a very strict Hindu, thought he was just out playing with friends.

Then his family moved to another neighborhood, and for the next three years he had no contact with Christian friends. In India when you reach the end of your 10th year, you take a very important week long test where you write out answers to many questions. This is the turning point for children in India, determining what path they will take depending on their test grades. You need to achieve a 60% or above to go on to being a doctor or lawyer for example.

Two weeks before this test, Solomon broke his finger on his right hand. The doctor said he would not be able to write for the exam. However, his mother was able to arrange for someone to write the answers for him. More importantly, she also took a 14 hour trip to a place called the Christian Prayer Tower where there were many miracles, signs and wonders happening and many answers to prayer. His mother was not a Christian, but heard about the amazing things happening here. She wanted prayer for her son to have his finger healed. After returning from her trip, The Prayer Tower sent her son a letter. When he opened it, Solomon saw many

Scriptures which he remembered from three years ago, and something strengthened in his spirit! This is where his life made a turn.

The bandages were removed from his finger, and he was able to write for his exam. He said that he was full of confidence from the Scriptures, and he passed the test with good marks. It was then he started to go to a Baptist Church. This caused much tension in his house with his father. His father actually told him to leave one night as he returned from church, however his mother did let him in the back door. She asked him not to go to church unless his father was away on business.

That night he prayed so earnestly to God for faith for his whole family. He asked his whole church to pray for his father because at his church there were many healings and miracles happening. Within one week, his father had terrible chest pains. Young Solomon went to his father and prayed and rubbed oil over his father while his father labored to breathe. His father could not speak or see what was happening, but he slowly slipped into sleep.

The next day they took him to the hospital, and the doctors reported he was totally normal. His father called Solomon and asked him if he prayed for him, and his son said he had. His father told him how he felt a cool breeze coming down over his head to his heart. He said that he felt the terrible pain go away.

Sunday came and you could hear the singing from the Baptist church right in the living room of their house. His father heard it and asked his son if he wanted to go to church. Solomon was so excited. His father said, "Here is some money to give the church." He now had the freedom to go to church. At the church's annual convention meeting, young Solomon formally gave his life to Jesus Christ. He started praying for his family which included his brother who was miraculously healed from a disease. This brother also accepted the Lord, and at the next annual convention, the two brothers were both baptized in water. Then together they prayed for their family, and their youngest sister came to accept Christ. Then the three prayed, and their mother became a Christian. Even their father left the Hindu religion and also accepted Jesus as Lord. Another sister followed. Solomon said that in a period of four and a half years because of prayer, all his family came to a saving faith in Jesus!!

CRUCIAL PRAYERS

Author, Randall D. Roth, writes, "While I am not an expert on prayer, I am an answer to prayer. Only later in my life did I learn that I was the object of the prayers of godly grandparents. My Grandpa Charlie told me that Grandma Ollie, both now with the Lord, would rise daily at 5:30 am, roll out of bed and onto her knees." His grandmother had a prayer list, and he was on it. He said the "Hound of Heaven" caught up with him when he was a freshman in high school, after some quite rebellious years. He says that those prayers are why he is where he is today. (*Prayer Powerpoints,* p.11)

One Sunday, a great evangelist, Dwight Thompson, was the guest speaker at our church in Fort Myers, Florida. I still remember this service so well. Our church was replacing the old seats with new comfortable ones, and only one section was ready for people to sit in. My husband marches us right up to the front row of this small section of seats and we sit down. I felt somewhat uncomfortable since this is where the pastors usually sit, but now I am glad we sat just there. Our church took up a collection for the new seating weeks prior to this, and Charlie, my husband, had contributed for five seats, two for us and one for each of our sons! From the front row, I heard this powerful man of God, who has brought many to the Lord through his dedicated life say, "I would not be here today if it were not for the prayers of my mother!" My eyes flooded. I just could not stop the tears! It was such an encouragement to me that someday, my sons would be saying these same words, and they too would be doing great things for God.

God seemed to always give me just the right encouragement to keep going—keep praying. One thing that motivated me was what Chip Ingram, President of Living on the Edge ministry, wrote in his book, *The Invisible War*. He explained how intercessory prayer is "crucial" for people to accept the gospel. "There is a connection between people praying and the ability of those for whom they pray to see. When people are coming to Christ, I can guarantee you that somewhere, somehow, someone believes in prayer—and is actually doing it, not just talking about it." (p.38) Seven things you can pray for others to receive Jesus as Lord are that:

    1) the spirits of darkness be removed from them.
    2) God would open the eyes of their understanding.
    3) the Holy Spirit would draw them close.
    4) God would renew their nature.
    5) laborers come across their path.
    6) God would move their wills to receive Jesus.
    7) God would work everything necessary needed to bring them to salvation.

If you are a born again believer in Jesus Christ, who prayed for you? Something to think about and someone to thank! Thank God for putting you on that person's heart!

Paul said to Timothy, "I have been reminded of your sincere faith, which first lived in your grandmother Lois and in your mother Eunice, and I am persuaded now lives in you" (2 Tim.1:5). Paul was saying that Timothy's faith did not start with him, but from a grandmother and mother who honored God with their lives. They prayed for Timothy, and God blessed them with passing their faith down to the next generation. They sacrificed with their prayers and life, and God honored their efforts. Our lives affect generations! Your faith may have come from many generations past if you do not see it in your parents or grandparents. After he was saved, my son Brian sent me a card which included this verse. He knows that God honored the prayers of his grandmother and his mother just like Timothy! He recognized that his faith in God was an answer to prayer!

  Recently I had another birthday. What a blessing from the Lord to receive a birthday card from my two sons traveling in ministry. One of them wrote these words, "Thank you for <u>All</u> you do and for praying us in!" My other son's message included these words, "Thank you for all your love and prayer that brought us into the Kingdom of God." Now, these words I will always treasure in my heart. They are not only saved and delivered, but thankful to me for the countless hours and years of prayer. I received a double blessing! In Isaiah 61:7 we read, "Instead of shame and dishonor, you will enjoy a double share of honor" (NLT). Psalm 40:1 reads, "I waited patiently for the Lord to help me, and he turned to me and heard my cry!" (NLT). I give thanks to the Lord for His faithfulness, His mercy, and His grace! Are your prayers worth it? YES!!! And for my sons', "Thank Yous"!!! All worth it—like the song lyrics to, "It Was Worth It All"...

> It was worth it all. It was worth it all.
> The pain that I've been through, it was worth it all. A soul's been saved. A life's been rearranged.
> Everything I've been through. It was worth it all.

(Mississippi Mass Choir, "It Was Worth It All". Album: Not By Might, Not By Power. 2005.
www.youtube.com/watch?v=iMAMvlkOfSc)

Chapter 5

PRAY THE WORD!

"For I am watching over My word to perform it."
Jeremiah 1:12 (NASB)

A Way of Escape

In January of 2006, I moved to Fort Myers, Florida with my son Shane, while my husband commuted back and forth from Chicago maintaining a business. Shane was going to finish up his last three semesters of high school at a Christian High School there in Florida. My oldest son was beginning his second year of college in Champaign, Illinois, and my middle son was starting college at Olivet Nazarene University. It all sounds quite normal and good. It was not. We were moving down to Fort Myers to get away from a public high school environment which ended in lifestyles of drugs, alcohol, rehabs, police and a totally dysfunctional family! I also thought it would be good for our marriage which was another part of our dysfunction. Marriage counseling on top of family and drug-addiction counseling was now a part of our schedule.

How this move transpired is that it started with a "For Sale" sign in the front yard of our house. We were going to simply move to a smaller, more manageable house in the same neighborhood. One day a friend of mine called and said that she saw the sign and wanted to let me know that she was also moving. She suggested that we follow them and move to Fort Myers, Florida! I said to her, "No way! I am not moving to Fort Myers, I don't know anyone down there!" She would not let me go until she told the whole story. She said that they went down to Florida and found a great Christian high school. I still did not know how that had anything to do with us. Then she said that Shane, my son who was a friend of her son, wanted to go also! I started to listen.

I wanted Shane to go to the Christian high school in our area from the beginning. He was all signed up to go there his freshman year, and we even had the down payment in. However, he gave us so much grief about going there, well I would say that he was "relentless", that eventually we let him go to the public school. So now, when my friend said this, she had my attention. This environment we were in was not working! I felt such a heaviness, and I actually envisioned carrying the weight of all four men on my back. I would describe our home as "very sad." God promises in his Word that "God is faithful, who will not allow you to be tempted beyond what you are able, but with the temptation will provide the way of escape also, so that you will be able to endure it" (1Cor.10:13, NASB).

Was this it? Was this the way of escape? It must have been the Holy Spirit reminding me of a story I once heard about James Dobson. It was about how his father moved to a different town because James was not going in the right direction in the environment he was in. It worked for them! I felt strongly that God was directing us to make this change. It was really a huge move, but when you hear God, He gives you the strength to do it. Of course, Charlie had no problem with Florida! But in the middle of all this, I started to have questions. I asked God again, "Why are we doing this?" He reminded me, "So Shane could go to a Christian High School." That was good enough. He did not tell me the "more to His story" at that time. This move was to be more about Charlie than my son Shane. It was not easy, but we moved!

I have always felt that my story had similarities to the story of Abraham where God told Abraham to move (Genesis 12:1). It comforted me to think about it! It was a pretty daring move and a major change, but we needed nothing short of it. We needed something major to happen. We needed miracles! I think of how God used all the pain, heaviness and confusion going on in my home and heart, to make this happen. It lead us right into the hands of God's loving way that would bring my husband home to Him. Only God knew that Charlie's time on earth was short.

My husband needed to be rescued from the enemy, and God made great use of the time Charlie had left. First He had to move us! God told Abraham to go. He was going to make him into a great nation. God told me to go. He was working on saving my family. I gained strength from Abraham's obedience. "The Lord had said to Abram, 'Leave your native country, your relatives, and your father's family, and go to the land that I will show you' " (Gen.12:1, NLT).

Taped to my mirror on an index card is this verse which still encourages me today: "Abraham believed God, and it was counted to him as righteousness" (Romans 4:3). Little did I know or understand at this time that God was working on and setting up *His Miracle Number One*... perfectly, patiently, precisely. He was hearing me all the time. He cared for me, my husband and my three sons.

Prayers That Get Results

Once in Fort Myers I started going to a women's Bible study on Monday nights called, "Help for Hurting Women". I qualified. At the end of the meeting on that first night I attended, anyone that wanted prayer was invited to come forward. I went forward for prayer for the four men in my family. The women's pastor prayed for me, my husband and sons. I could not stop crying. The burden had been so much for so long. I was hurting, and I just needed God. Period! She was so kind and asked me if I had the book, <u>Prayers That Avail Much.</u> I said that I did not, so she gave me a copy of one that night. It was a book full of prayers that pray God's Word in almost every line. This was the beginning of my feeling I had found some thing or some way that God would hear and help me! I found new hope! I began reading and learning about how to pray God's Word. In her book, Germaine Copeland says the kind of prayer that gets results must be based upon the Word of God.

> Prayer is not to be a religious form with no power. It is to be effective and accurate and brings results. God watches over His Word to perform it (Jer. 1:12).... Talk the answer, not the problem. The answer is in God's Word... Prayer must be the foundation of every Christian endeavor. Any failure is a prayer failure. We are not to be ignorant concerning God's Word... Using God's Word on purpose, specifically, in prayer is one means of prayer, and it is a most effective and accurate means. (xvii-xxi)

This study brought new revelation to how I prayed and a new confidence that my prayers would get results. The Word of God is the revealed will of God, so if I prayed His will, my prayer was heard. 1John 5:14-15 reads, "This is the confidence we have in approaching God: that if we ask anything according to his will, he hears us. And if we know that he hears us—whatever we ask—we know that we have what we asked of him." I first had to study the Word for my situation and have faith in it. "Faith comes by hearing, and hearing by the Word of God" (Romans 10:17, NKJV). Then I was able to pray and confess the Word over the situation. I was learning to abide in His Word! Jesus said, "If you abide in me and my words abide in you, ask whatever you wish, and it will be done for you" (John 15:7, NASB). These were not empty words, but God's Word becoming part of my life.

God's Word will produce results because we are in contact with Him through His Word. When we put God in remembrance of His Word (Isaiah 43:26), He says that, "It shall not return to Me void, But it shall accomplish what I please, and it shall prosper in the thing for which I sent it" (Isaiah 55:11, NKJV). Present God with His Word, and It will do what It says. His Word has power and It has life. John 6:63 says, "The words that I speak to you are spirit, and they are life" (NKJV). Speaking God's Word creates and has the power to produce. "By the word of the Lord the heavens were made, and all the host of them by the breath of His mouth" (Psalms 33:6, NKJV). The universe was brought into existence by His spoken Word and the Spirit of God! "In the beginning was the Word, and the Word was with God, and the Word was God. He was with God in the beginning. All things were made through him, and without him nothing was made that was made" (John 1:1-3, NKJV). Author Derek Prince writes, "Every Word of God contains within it the power for its own fulfillment." (*Secrets of a Prayer Warrior,* p. 53)

SPEAK OUT THE WORD

I learned that I needed to get God's Word coming from "my" mouth. Mark Hankins, preacher and author, says..."the devil would fight against you getting the Word in your mouth. Everything Jesus did is activated by getting the Word in your mouth and in your heart. Reinhard Bonnke said the Lord told him, 'My Word in your mouth is just as powerful as My Word in My mouth.' " (*The Spirit of Faith,* p.56) God watches over His Word coming from my mouth and then does it. Jeremiah 1:12 says, "Then the Lord said to me, You have seen well, for I am alert and active, watching over My word to perform it" (AMP). His Word is even above His name as we read, "For You have magnified Your word above all Your name"(Psalm 138:2b, NKJV). And, His Word is forever set in Heaven. Jesus said, "Heaven and earth shall pass away, but my words shall not pass away" (Matt. 24:35, KJV). God's Word is settled in heaven and will last forever.

I feel that up to this time, I did more talking about the problem than talking about the answer. So no wonder things stayed the same. I was getting what I spoke. God wants results, and these results come from agreeing with and praying His Word. An angel of the Lord brought Mary a Word ordained by God and she asked, "How will this be?" (Luke 1:34). When Mary agreed with the Word spoken over her, "Let it be done to me according to what you have said" (Luke 1:38, AMP), it happened! When Mary agreed with the Word, power was released, and the Word was fulfilled. Mary became pregnant with God's Son. God says, "For I am the Lord; I will speak, and the word that I shall speak shall be performed... I will speak the word and will perform it, says the Lord God" (Eze. 12:25, AMP). When we speak out God's Word and agree with it, angels are waiting and ready to carry the Word to its assignment. "Bless the Lord, you His angels, Mighty in strength, who perform His word, Obeying the voice of His word" (Psalm 103:20, NASB). All I had around me until this time were Mighty yawning angels, waiting for me to speak His Word. They wanted to be sent out with the answer. Mark Hankins says, "When you get the Word in your mouth, you have the answer. The answer is already in the Word!" (*The Spirit of Faith,* p.56) Speak out the promise of God for your situation. Receive it and receive the power for it to be fulfilled. "For nothing is impossible with God" (Luke 1:37).

In his book, Mark Hankins talks about winning your war with words. "Never run at your giant with your mouth shut! We must win the war of words before we win in any area of life. God has supplied the ammunition, the Word, to win in every area....You are a believer, and you must speak what you believe for victory to be yours." (*Spirit of Faith,* p.48-55) With every trial or situation we face, there is a Word in the Bible for it, and when we speak it out, power is released. Before David fought Goliath, they battled with words. David won because he had the last word, "...The Lord saveth not with sword and spear: for the battle is the Lord's and he will give you into our hands" (1 Samuel 17:47, KJV). Before the fight started, David won. He had faith in what he believed and spoke. I believe that stone traveled right along the path of that spoken word and landed right in the forehead of Goliath for the victory. When you are battling a giant in your life, open your mouth and attack it with God's Word. God has a word to defeat every one of your giants!

We must meditate on the Word, study the Word, and do the Word. When people see our lives, they should be reading the Bible! They should read you winning over temptation, abiding in Him, intimate with your Father, serving others, praying, worshiping, and His will being done through you, including miracles! Jerry Savelle, Christian author, writes, "Be so devoted to the Word that you get addicted to it. Get to the point in your spiritual life where you cannot get enough of the Word. When you pray the Prayer of Petition and stand on God's Word and allow it to saturate your soul, there is no way the devil—or anyone or anything else—can keep you from experiencing the answer to your prayer." (*Prayer of Petition,* p.152)

Kay Arthur, a very respected Bible teacher, believes that the greatest book there is on prayer is the Bible. You cannot be weak in the Word and strong in prayer. She writes, "If your knowledge of Scripture is shallow, your prayers will be too." (*Lord, Teach Me to Pray in 28 Days,* p.58) We should devote our time to study the Word to know His will and His promises. Then we will be able to say, "Do as you have said"

(1Chron. 17: 23, NKJV). Author Derek Prince explains it well, "Lord, You said it, please do it. If God has said He will do it, and you ask Him to do it, you can *know* He is going to do it. His promises are the revelation of His will." (*Secrets of a Prayer Warrior,* p. 52) However, remember that our motive must be that God's name be glorified! Revelation of His will glorifies Him. Miracles bring Him glory!

*****

Do you have a giant to slay or a miracle to receive? What are your angels doing? Are they yawning or working? For the glory of God, receive His Word then speak it out. The power of the spoken Word with the Spirit will bring LIFE to your promise!

Chapter 6

DO MY PRAYERS EVEN MATTER?

"God will do nothing on earth except in answer to believing prayer." John Wesley

One very big question I had in the midst of all my prayers and pleas was, "Do my prayers even matter?" If God is in control, what part do my prayers play? I could not see any results from the way I was praying, so I needed an answer to this. God knew that! "For your Father knows exactly what you need even before you ask him!" (Matthew 6:8, NLT). I asked someone at my church what they recommended as a good book on prayer. She said that Dutch Sheets was a good author on that subject. At the bookstore I found his book, *Intercessory Prayer, How God Can Use Your Prayers to Move Heaven and Earth.* There was no question that I needed heaven moved and earth moved! I needed a mountain moving excavation bulldozer! This book changed me and my confidence in prayer! He wrote and answered, "When God says, 'pray,' I want to know it will matter. . . Is prayer really necessary? The real question is: Does a sovereign, all-powerful God need our involvement or not? Is prayer really necessary? If so, why?" (p.23)

God tells us to "pray without ceasing" and to pray for "God's will to be done", but the question remains, is God going to do what He wants anyway? If God is sovereign, how do my prayers fit in? The answer to this lies in how God created the earth and how He set things in order. God created the earth; He owns it. However, He gave management of it to man. In Genesis 1:26 God said, "Let us make man in Our image, according to Our likeness; and let them rule over the fish of the sea and over the birds of the sky and over the cattle and over all the earth, and over every creeping thing that creeps on the earth" (NASB). Psalm 115:16 tells us, "The highest heavens belong to the Lord, but the earth he has given to mankind." After man sinned, God showed that he wanted to work with the earth through humans by becoming a man Himself to rescue them. The way that God can work His will on the earth is through getting permission from man to do it. Man does this through prayer. God "the owner" works His will on the earth through the requests of the "managers." In his book, Sheets writes, "Here we have, I believe, the reason for the necessity of prayer. God chose, from the time of the Creation, to work on the earth through humans, not independent of them... He always has and always will, even at the cost of becoming one. Though God is sovereign and all-powerful, Scripture clearly tells us that He limited Himself, concerning the affairs of earth, to working through human beings." (*Intercessory Prayer*, p. 28-29)

This means that God can be limited. We limit God because of our free will which He gave to man. God has His good and perfect will, but He will not intrude into man's will unless invited. Watchman Nee confirms, "God is in heaven, yet all His movements on earth must first be decided and agreed upon by the will on earth. God will not ignore the will on earth, nor will He take away and work independently." (*Burden and Prayer,* p.13) God works through the prayers of His people, because this is the means God put into place to bring down His plan to earth according to His will. We partner with God through praying His will to earth. God has so much more that He wants to see come to earth. His will is "not wanting anyone to perish, but everyone to come to repentance" (2Peter 3:9b). We as Christians limit God through not obeying his command to "pray without ceasing" (1Thes. 5:17 KJV). God has "so much more" (Matt. 7:11, KJV) to give, but we do not ask or pray for it. He tells us to "Command ye me" as in Isaiah 45:11 God says, "Thus saith the Lord, the Holy One of Israel, and his Maker, Ask me of things to come concerning my sons; and concerning the work of my hands, command ye me"(KJV). What God is saying is that He is the only one that can do anything about what is needed, so come to Him. John 15:5 reads, "For without me, ye can do nothing" (KJV). The only way we can do anything is to do it through the power of God. When God says to command Him, we are still asking Him. We are asking Him, and reminding Him of what His Word says. He did not forget, but God wants to build our own faith up by hearing what He has said! However, know that for something to be accomplished, God is the only One capable, so we command Him to do it.

God's people on earth must act before heaven can move. We must act in prayer. Author E. M. Bounds writes, "God rests the very life and prosperity of His cause on prayer. . . . Prayer became the settled and only condition to move His Son's kingdom." (*Understanding Prayer,* p. 10-11) God already has set what His purpose is for earth, but earth must contact heaven for it to move forward. Man has free will to choose, and our loving Father so much desires for us to make the right choice, Him! He gives us two choices, but also gives us the answer. "I have set before you life and death, blessings and curses. Now choose life so that you and your children may live" (Deut. 30:19). When the desire of man on earth comes into agreement with the desire of God, and when man's will matches God's will, miracles take place. (Charlie's miracle, Brian's miracle, and Colin's miracle) This is the glory of God! Miracles show forth God's glory.

Knowing that God moves Heaven to Earth through our prayers, we have an essential part in God's plan for all to come to a saving faith. Our prayers mean life and death to people. Would you not agree that it is essential that we believers "pray without ceasing, ask and keep asking, and knock and keep knocking?" (1Thess. 5:17, Matt.7:7). Prayer is not a suggestion; it is a command. Bill Johnson tells it like this, "We are His delegated authority on planet earth, and prayer is the vehicle that gives occasion for His invasion. Those who don't pray allow darkness to continue ruling." (*When Heaven Invades Earth,* p. 64) We pray His will to be done to show His glory throughout the earth. It is work, it is ministry, and it is our responsibility. It is also a privilege to be working along side God, to be an ambassador of Christ and to know our prayers touch His heart. Yes! My prayers matter! God did an amazing job of answering my question. He kept leading me forward on our "prayer journey". This was a very big step in my *prayer warrior boot camp.*

Chapter 7

PRAYER DEPENDS ON YOUR LIFE

"My prayer will depend on my life." Andrew Murray

Prayer changes things. Prayer changes you. It certainly has changed me. It really began the day I first called out to God after picturing myself up in heaven on "that day", and what if He said to me, "I never knew you, depart from me!" (Matt. 7:23, NASB). I asked God to, "Do something! If I don't have the kind of faith to get in, do something!" I did not want to spend my life thinking I had my admission ticket to heaven in my hand, but all I really was holding was still an invitation. David Platt, pastor and New York Times bestselling author, says, quoting from Matt.7:21, "*I never knew you.* Is that possible? Is it possible for you or me to profess to be a Christian and yet not know Christ? Absolutely. And according to Jesus, it's actually *probable*." (*Follow Me,* p.7) I think I was lukewarm and deceived. God says in Revelation 3:16, "So, because you are lukewarm, neither cold nor hot, I will vomit you out of my mouth!" (NKJV) Those words from God did not sound pleasant. I was lukewarm, doing church and Bible study, and then doing my own life: mom, housekeeper, wife, cheerleader and friend. God used His Word to convict me. I had a holy fear of God, and I did not ignore Him, Praise God! He says, "Today if you hear his voice, do not harden your hearts as in rebellion" (Hebrews 3:15, ESV).

God's Classroom: Kneepads Required!

God was faithful and loving and responded to my invitation, "Do something!" He allowed something to happen.

My life fell on me like an avalanche! I was forced to my knees, the place God needed me to be so He could start to work. He had my attention and my permission to begin to build the "good work" in me. It is what God needs to change you. You need to give Him a work permit so He can start His construction project! God finishes what He starts. He says that, "Being confident of this, that He who began a good work in you will carry it onto completion until the day of Christ Jesus" (Phil. 1:6). Sometimes I have actually asked, "God, aren't you done yet?"

God has been extremely busy teaching me all about Him and "His Ways". He signed me up for many of His classes. These were one-on-one instructional classes between me and the Holy Spirit. Our classroom settings included a crisis, a storm, and a valley. The classes were:

- Seek First the Kingdom of God: Change Your Priorities
- I Am a Jealous God: Drop Your Idols
- A Quiet and Gentle Spirit Class: Don't Say a Word
- Be Submissive: So They May be Won Over
- I Hate Divorce: Write a Fireproof Curriculum
- Do Not Be Offended: Forgive Seventy plus Seven Times
- Leave Home: Go to the Land I Will Show You
- Widow: I'm Your Husband
- Be Anxious for Nothing: Trust Me
- The Abraham Class: Give Me Your Son
- The Esther Class— For Such a Time as This: Let's Roll!
- I Have a Plan For You: Game On!
- Shut the Door: Let's Talk!
- Lord Teach Me to Pray: 101,102,103

There are many more classes I have yet to take and many I have had to repeat!

A.W. Tozer says it this way:

> We might well pray for God to invade and conquer us, for until He does, we remain in peril from a thousand foes. We bear within us the seeds of our own disintegration...The strength of our flesh is an ever present danger to our souls. Deliverance can come to us only by the defeat of our old life. Safety and peace come only after we have been forced to our knees...So He conquers us and by that benign conquest saves us for Himself. (*The Christian Quote Book,* Quillin, p.74)

As Followers of Jesus, we are to go to the Word and learn what God says about each circumstance or situation. God changes us as we learn to handle life His way, and we are responsible to do what He commands. God's Word has an answer for every problem. The answers are not usually easy, but they are the only answers for significant and lasting change. Graham Cooke, Christian speaker and author, says that in each of these problems, God has an "upgrade" for you. You will mature spiritually if you do not waste the circumstance by going through it your own way.

It is hard to kill the flesh, but each step of obedience makes the next step easier. It is like learning to speak a foreign language—the language of the Kingdom. Because I have not been able to get off my knees, God has done a good job in keeping me in His classroom. I am in His Continuing Education Program, as we all need to be. He tells us in His Word exactly what He is doing, "...God, who began the good work within you, will continue his work until it is finally finished on the day when Christ Jesus returns" (Phil. 1:6,NLT).

While I am here on this side of heaven, He will keep building His good work in me. Actually, I think that God does not have any seats in his classroom, only knee pads! We cannot learn sitting down or standing up!

Avalanche!

I still remember a day in church more than twenty years ago, when we were singing a song with the lyrics, "I am down on my knees in my heart." My husband, Charlie, said, "I am sitting down on my butt in my heart!" I thought that comment was odd, surprising, and just strange, but now I see where his heart was at that time. It took over twenty years for God to get him to his knees. An avalanche had to fall on him, too!

A huge part of that avalanche hit him when his sister-in-law called, and she "let him have it!" Charlie had told me something about Mary Lu— that she did not like me. I thought that was odd, and so I called her and asked her about this. She became so angry at Charlie, that he would say such a lie to hurt me. We had a three way phone conversation going, and I listened as she told him how he had been so selfish all his life. She had known my husband when he was in high school, during his rebellious years. She went on and on about how selfish he was. She went through story after story. It was excruciatingly painful for me to listen to, and I began to hurt for my husband. She was extremely rough on him! He actually hung up and then picked the phone back up again. He was having a very hard time hearing this. After that phone call, we did not talk about it until the next day. Eventually, Charlie asked me about the call and what I thought. I said, "I felt so bad for you. She was really rough. But, what she said was true." Avalanche! I really, truly feel Charlie fell to his knees in his heart that day. When he was baptized only months later, he said that he had been selfish and wanted to apologize to his wife and his family and to God. This came partly as a result of that phone conversation. Thank you, Lord, for my sister-in-law, Mary Lu. I think it was life changing, humbling, and necessary for Charlie to fall to his knees. Time was running out. God used all things to work together for good, including this phone call.

Charlie Gets To Class!

Charlie's life started changing. God was working on the inside, and we could see it on the outside. Brian, my son, told my mother that Dad was acting nicer toward me. Pastor Grant saw a big change and told me at church, "Charlie is changing!" Charlie even started serving at the church, and he also wanted to grow spiritually. He picked up a Christian book and read it in one sitting. The name of it was *Rescued*, by John Bevere. He started reading the book at 10 at night and read until 3 in the morning. It ironically was about a Pastor of a church who was deceived about his own walk with the Lord. Pastor Rockaway thought he was saved, but his life did not line up with God's will. He divorced his wife for his soul mate, had a big mega church which was just about his ego, and his life was all about himself, not God. It took a crisis, being trapped at the bottom of the ocean in a submarine, for God to get his attention. It was there, at that moment, he was convicted of his sin and he saw his life for what it really was—one of deceit and lies from the enemy. He called out to God and was saved just before he died. I think of Charlie's story and this story having many similarities. Charlie could not put the book down, and it was the last book Charlie read.

Change? Can you see it?

God says in His Word that if you are a follower of His, your life should look different. "I have been crucified with Christ. It is no longer I who live, but Christ who lives in me. The life I live in the Body, I live by faith in the Son of God, who loved me and gave himself for me" (Galatians 2:20). If our old self is dead, taken to the cross, and our new self lives in unity with Him, there has got to be a changed life inside and visible on the outside. We go through a process of sanctification, where we become more and more like Christ as we renew our minds with the Word of God. We read that as followers, "We have put on the new self, which is being renewed in knowledge in the image of its Creator" (Col. 3:10).

We change as we go through this lifelong process of learning and obeying, and our will is transformed to match His will. This is done through meditating on God's Word as He says in Joshua 1:8a, "Do not let this Book of the Law depart from your mouth; meditate on it day and night, so that you may be careful to do everything written in it." God's Word is God's will. We are to pray God's will, and we can do this by having our wills transformed by reading the Word. He changes our will to His will. Romans 12:2 says, "Do not conform any longer to the pattern of this world, but be transformed by the renewing of your mind. Then you will be able to test and approve what God's will is—his good, pleasing and perfect will." People can change their behavior, but it takes the Holy Spirit to work deeper in us so that we are transformed in our attitudes of the heart. The Holy Spirit and the Word of God change our selfish, anxious, prideful and stubborn hearts. "If you abide in me, and my words abide in you, ask whatever you wish, and it will be done for you" (John 15:7, NASB). God's condition to answered prayer is that *we* have changed! We have put on the mind of Christ. We are abiding in Him, and His Word is in us which has changed our will to match His will.

Andrew Murray sums it up like this: "As the words of Christ enter our very hearts, becoming and influencing our lives, our words will enter His heart and influence Him. My prayer will depend on my life: Whatever God's words are to me and in me will determine what my words will be to God and in God. If I do what God says, God will do what I say." (*With Christ in the School of Prayer,* p.165) I like what Leonard Ravenhill says, "A sinning man will stop praying. A praying man will stop sinning." (*The Christian Quote Book,* Quillin p.73)

We may have people in our lives that we have been praying for, for years. However, the primary purpose of prayer is to change us. Then, as we change, our prayers can change and our circumstances change. In his book, *The Circle Maker*, a book on prayer, Mark Batterson tells a story about a great evangelist, Rodney "Gypsy" Smith, who has preached the gospel to millions. His secret to his preaching was his private prayer. He told a group of people, who wanted to preach and have influence like him, what to do. He said to take a piece of chalk, go into a room, lock it, and draw a circle on the floor with the chalk. Then, kneel in the circle. "There on your knees, pray fervently and brokenly that God would start a revival with that chalk circle." (p. 215) We need to have revival start in us! We need an intimacy with God. God needs to change us first, before we can influence others for Him. Invite God to, "Search me, O God, and know my heart; test me and know my anxious thoughts. See if there is any offensive way in me, and lead me in the way everlasting" (Psalm139:23-24). This is giving God our building permit so He can start construction. For things to change, we have to change; for things to be different we have to be different. A real intimate relationship with the Father through Jesus Christ, followed by allowing God to mature us through meditating on the Word, is what makes the difference.

Author, Andrew Murray, blames unanswered prayer on our feeble lives! "Disciples of Christ! While we have been excusing our unanswered prayers with a fancied submission to God's wisdom and will, the real reason has been that our own feeble lives have been the cause of our feeble prayers! Nothing can make men strong but the Word coming from God's mouth." (*With Christ in the School of Prayer,* p.166) A feeble life is a spiritually weak life which results in praying weak prayers. We must become strong and mature in our faith, and this is done in degrees. The Word says that we are changed by looking in the Word and are, "constantly being transfigured into His very own image in ever increasing splendor and from one degree of glory to another... by the Spirit" (2Cor.3:18, AMP).

*****

God keeps maturing us step by step. Everyone should know what step God is working on in them: "The Word of God, which is effectually at work in you who believe [exercising its superhuman power in those who adhere to and trust in and rely on it]" (1Th. 2:13, AMP). We read the Word and the Word reads us. What in your life is God pointing out to you that your life is not lining up with His Word? This is the step He has you on right now. Not to worry! He does not have you work on everything at once. However, He will be patient and continue to work with you until you pass the test! Again, not to worry! If you do not pass the test, you get to do it over. Since all Disciples of Christ are in a continual education program, what class does God have you in? You need to know this, because God is waiting on you. It could be the class you need to pass, to be able to pray for a miracle. Get to class!

Chapter 8

PRAY IN SECRET

*"But you, when you pray, enter into your closet and when you shut your door, pray to your Father which is in secret, and your Father who sees in secret
shall reward you openly."(Matt.6:6, NKJ)*

The first thing that my two sons learned to do when they started traveling in ministry was to meet with their Father in secret. They spend much time in their prayer closet in the presence of God. They are rebuilding their lives. One of the truths they are learning is to spend time with the Father who is found always waiting in the secret place for them. They are now teaching me things about intimacy with God and praying for me!! My third son, Shane, said that he doesn't know anyone as dedicated to the Lord as his two brothers! He sees them always finding time to be alone with God. Shane sees his brothers totally changed through their new relationship with Jesus. First hand, he is a witness, "that anyone who belongs to Christ has become a new person. The old life is gone; a new life has begun" (2 Co. 5:17, NLT). He has seen Damascus Road experiences in both his brothers.

Two Miracles!

When Shane was in junior high, he wrote a paper titled, "Learning the Hard Way." It was an essay about how he does not have to learn the hard way, because he watched how his brother Brian's poor choices had caused him and his family so much grief. He would avoid learning the hard way himself. Shane watched things get worse.

On Shane's sixteen birthday, we had a party for him at our house. It was a good party, no drinking, no drugs, just a pleasant time. As the party was coming to an end and kids were leaving, the doorbell rang. It was the police. I thought, "Great! What was going on here that I did not know about? Had some kids left from here and gotten into trouble?" The police were not there for the party, but for Brian. He had gotten into a confrontation at the local Taco Bell and punched someone who had made fun of him about the cigarette lodged above his ear. The police were called, and my son and a friend of his were on the run. The police were looking for him, but so was God! This was nothing new for us. There was already a list of counselors, police, suspensions and rehabs. I later learned all these wrong choices were his way of dealing with inner pain and rejection. However, at this time things got worse.

One night, Shane accompanied me to the emergency room while the doctor put eighteen stitches in Brian's hand and fingers. That night, Charlie was out of town, and Colin was in the back of the yard with a bottle of alcohol. It was late, and Brian, who had given up alcohol at this time so he could start college at a Christian University, said, "Mom, go to bed, I know what to do, I will handle it." About thirty minutes later, I heard a loud crash, came downstairs and saw a towel covered in blood wrapped around Brian's hand. He had started drinking and was very intoxicated. He got angry at himself and put his hand through a pane of glass in the library door. Colin offered to drive him to the hospital! Right! Shane and I took Brian to the Emergency Room, and we watched as the doctor sewed up his hand. God protected him from any nerve damage. God was helping in even little details including finding a way to replace the shattered imported pane of glass from Italy. He helped me find the answer in a craft store in a neighboring town, and I thought, Italy! God has surely protected us from so much, because from here, things got much worse.

Brian attended Olivet Nazarene University for a semester, which ended in a trip to the hospital in an ambulance followed by five days of detox. Things got worse. He switched from alcohol to drugs. He struggled through two semesters at another school, which ended with my husband having to quickly help rescue him and bring him home. Our home was now in Florida. Things got worse. In Florida, the drug to easily get was a prescription pain killer, oxycotin. Brian's addiction became a $30.00 to $100.00 a day habit.

One evening when Brian was going to a class at a local community college, I received a text from him. It said, "I need to see a doctor." When he came home, he told me about his addiction. Before class, he said he was in the car, using a needle to shoot this drug into his arm. He started to feel horrible about what he was doing and had a "came to his senses" moment. Brian said that God showed up in the car that night, and he felt God's tangible presence. (I found this out much later.) Brian wanted to make a change. It was not easy for him to get from that night to traveling in ministry, but God got hold of him. With God, ALL things are possible!

It was at Teen Challenge in Sandhills, North Carolina that Brian said he was called into ministry! This was a year long Christian-based rehab program. Shane and I went to Brian's four day visit together at Sandhills. I flew to Chattanooga, Shane picked me up, and we drove those seven hours together across the state. The next morning, as Shane and I drove up to the dorm, there was Brian anxiously waiting on the porch with one of the counselors. He looked so happy and healthy. It had been a long road for him from the night he sent me that text message until that day, which was then over two years. Shane and I had seen God work a miracle in Brian. I am so thankful to God and to God be the glory!

Last May, around the time of his graduation from college, Shane saw another total miracle take place before his eyes. A few weeks before the graduation, Colin drove down from Chicago and stayed with Shane for a week. Then Colin drove down to Mississippi to spend a few days with Brian and the ministry he was serving with. Brian had spent the last nine months traveling with this ministry, and Colin wanted to just check it out. The minister and Brian were simply going to show Colin love, however God moved in a mighty way. They met Colin in the bar of the hotel he was staying at. He was going to just order a drink and wait for them to show up. However, before having a chance to order a drink, the minister walked in with Brian. Right there, they prayed for Colin and laid hands on him, and God instantly delivered him from alcohol! Colin had given his life to the Lord three months earlier but was not yet delivered from this addiction. When Colin and Brian drove back for Shane's graduation, we witnessed a miracle! Shane had seen his brother just a week earlier, totally bound and now totally set free. Colin also decided to leave Chicago and travel with his brother and this ministry. God was breaking all the chains. I am so grateful to God and to God be the glory!

The Secret Place

My two sons, redeemed, restored and in ministry for the Lord, are rewards from my Father who saw me praying to Him for them in secret!! That verse in the Bible, Matthew 6:6, has been such an encouragement to me so many times to keep coming to Him for my sons. He sees me and He will reward me openly. He has!! And He will continue! One thing I have to do is meet with Him in secret, where He waits for me to show up.

One day my son, Brian, called and told me about a book he was reading and said it was the best book ever; that every chapter was amazing. He wanted me to get it for myself. The name of the book was, *Secrets of the Secret Place*, by Bob Sorge. Of course I got the book, and it really is amazing. However, more amazing to me is that this son was the one I would have to bribe with money to read Christian books. Now he was trying to get me to read a book so that I could grow in the things of God. Also, I am sure that the money he earned did not go to God-honoring purchases. I got this idea from the father of bestselling author John Maxwell. I read how he paid his son to get him to read Christian books. Now he writes them! It seemed like a great plan to me at the time. I tried so many ways to rescue my son from the path he was on. However, meeting with God in the secret place was one of the lessons I needed to learn! God had a better way than my way —bribery!

The first year after my husband died, I was alone in my house most of the year. My three sons were away at college so the entire house was my prayer closet. There were no distractions, interruptions, or people watching or listening. I got alone with God every day in many places in my house, on my patio, and sometimes I went over to the beach. I liked to pray by the water. In all these places, I was in God's presence. In his book, Bob Sorge says that "There is a guaranteed way to get into God's presence...a sure-fire 100% guaranteed way to have instant intimacy with the Father, and Jesus Himself gave us the key. ...The moment you get to the secret place, you are in the immediate presence of your Father." (*Secrets of the Secret Place*, p.8) He was referring to Matt. 6:6 which says "go into your secret room, and when you shut your door, pray to your Father who is in the secret place" (NKJV). He is in the secret place! All you have to do is show up.

Meeting with God, *alone*, is an essential and foundational part of a Christian's life. "When you build your life on the blessed intimacy of a secret place relationship with God, you are building on the rock."(*Secrets of the Secret Place,* p.8) The secret place is an exciting place to go! You know the Father is already there, and He is waiting for you. He knows all about you and what you need even before you ask. He will teach you how to pray. He will reward you just because you came. He sees you, He so wants one-on-one time with you, He loves you, He knows all your concerns, He wants to listen, He wants to speak, He wants to reveal himself to you, and He wants to reward you OPENLY by having your prayers answered. Does it get any better? Yes! He is ". . .able to do exceedingly abundantly above all that we ask or think according to his power that works in us" (Eph. 3:20, KJV). God has so much to give, but we can only get what we show up for in secret with Him. The more we seek Him, the more our intimacy grows. God promises us that, "You seek me, and find me, when you search for me with all your heart" (Jeremiah 29:13, NASB). He promises to let you find him, but it has to be with your whole heart. Nothing less will do for God to let you find Him the way he longs for you to find Him. He lovingly says, "Shut the door, spend time with me!"

We Limit God

Our Father wants to have so much more intimacy with us than we allow Him. We limit God by not showing up! We keep busy doing good things and reading good books, but not praying in secret and spending "all our heart time" with Him! Paul prayed that we would "grasp how wide and how long and how high and how deep is the love of Christ, and to know this love that surpasses knowledge—that you may be filled to the fullness of the measure of all the fullness of God" (Eph. 3:18-19). God wants to fill you with His fullness, but He is not going to give you what you cannot handle. Our capacity to have more of God is determined by our intimacy with God. This is so key to the Christian life. We need more intimacy, not religiosity.

Dr. Tony Evans, pastor, speaker, and author, gave a great illustration of this in a message he gave at a Spiritual Life Conference. He said that God will only give you as much of Him as you can handle. If you go to the ocean with a thimble, you can only get a thimble full of water. If you go with a glass, you can get a glass full. If you go with a bucket, a bucket full, and a barrel, a barrel full. However, the ocean has an unlimited resource of water to give you. In the same way, God is the ocean of love and Himself. He will only give you as much of Him as you are able to receive. Our capacity to receive more increases as we increase in our intimacy with Him. Evans called this "divine capacity". The more capacity, the more power and authority we have. Also, the capacity for Him that you develop here on earth, will reflect your rewards in heaven for all eternity. ("Intimacy with God." Spiritual Life Conference,2012,Dallas,TX.
http.//www.youtube.com/watch?v=APH3HVckbsw)

We need to draw near to God and develop intimacy which means to go to the secret place where the Father is waiting! We then increase our capacity to receive more from Him and have more authority. Then, our prayers will no longer be feeble prayers. Our prayers can bring the miracle!

Prayer is simply communication with God. As Christians, we are not just about following the commands of God, but having a real relationship with Him. This is why Christ had to go to the cross, to take away the sin that prevented us from having that relationship with the Father. In order to truly have a relationship, there must be communication. We need to talk and listen to our heavenly Father, not just obey Him. He wants real conversation. Bible teacher, Kay Arthur writes, "Though Scripture sets forth all of the goals and standards for everyday life in principle, it usually doesn't fill in the practical details. That's why we need to talk and listen to our heavenly Father." (*Lord, Teach Me to Pray in 28 Days,* p.6) Half of this communication is hearing from or listening to God. The other half is us talking to Him.

When we are in the prayer closet, we need to take turns talking. We talk and send prayers and praises up to God, and then He wants a turn to speak and send answers, encouragement, or directions down to us. Bob Sorge says, "Things don't change when I talk to God; things change when God talks to me....So the power of prayer is found, not in convincing God of my agenda, but in waiting upon Him to hear His agenda." (*Secrets of the Secret Place,* 11) Sometimes the answer will come down as an action on what to do and other times will be to "Be still and know that I am God." (Psalm 46:10). Many times the voice of God speaks to me in my spirit with a Scripture. Quite often God has said, "I will make a road in the wilderness!" and "I will perfect what concerns you." God wants us to hear Him. He says, "He who has ears to hear, let him hear!" (Matthew 13:9, NKJV). He says that if we are His, we hear His voice and follow Him. "My sheep hear My voice, and I know them and they follow Me" (John 10:27, NKJV). Do you hear his voice? Does He know you? Do you follow Him? We need to listen and discern his voice. This is called listening prayer.

Learning to Listen

Today, I find my secret place to be on a small sofa in my room. There I can spend time with God because I can get quiet and still. I am learning to listen. This is a new class the Holy Spirit has signed me up for, "Listening Prayer Class (remedial level)." I say remedial because I did not even know that I was supposed to let God have a turn to speak. Now I am learning that there are over twenty ways God speaks. What He says will always line up with Scripture.

There is so much more to hearing and experiencing God. Just ask my miracle sons Colin and Brian who are praying for me to experience more of God like they are! I am learning to **hear** and **experience** the different ways God speaks. The Holy Spirit is a great teacher, and this is such an exciting class. I even feel like I am "teacher's pet!" I have experienced God's voice through impressions, dreams, an inner voice, circumstances, Scripture, and an inner knowing. Another way I have found God to speak to me is through visions. I have been drawing the visions in a sketchbook that I keep in my prayer closet. Some have been amazing!

Last February, when I was desperately seeking God to free Colin from depression, I had the vision of Jesus opening up His arms and first Colin, my oldest, approaches Him from the left side, then Brian, my middle son comes up to Him in the center, and then Shane, my youngest, comes up to Jesus on the right. Jesus wrapped His arms around all of them. They came to Him one-by-one. This is the Scripture God gave me also, "For the revelation awaits an appointed time, it speaks of the end and it will not prove false. Though it linger, wait for it: it will certainly come and will not delay" (Hab.2:3). I heard God say, "It's a wrap! I won't leave anyone out. I finish what I start and complete my work." This is God's character and He wanted to encourage me.

Encouragement is the most common purpose for hearing a word from God. I would not have heard Him in any other place, but the secret place—our secret place. There are more visions I drew in my book, and I realize that these only came at a time that I was really seeking God and giving Him time to speak to me. Really seeking God and intently listening gave God the opportunity to encourage me in this way. I am looking forward to what more God has to say and what I will be drawing in my sketchbook in the future.

*****

When meeting with God in a quiet place, our prayer closet, we should meditate on something and not have an empty mind. It can be about an attribute of God, how good and loving He is, something we are thankful for, or on a Scripture He has spoken through our spirit. We are to rest in Him and learn to hear from Him which means part of the time is listening. Perry Stone, pastor and author, talks about our time with God in prayer is like a ladder which has two directions, up and down. He writes, "Your prayers and words are climbing the ladder. However, your answers will be sent from the heavenly temple to you, and it is important to have a spiritually trained ear to hear what the Spirit is saying to you. . . .Your secret place should be the command center for communicating with the Lord, meditating upon His Word." (*Opening the Gates of Heaven,* p.155, 160) God will speak to you.

*****

If you want an answer to prayer or if you want a miracle, go and find your secret place, close the door, and make sure you bring your whole heart. God will be so excited to see you!

VISION ENTRIES FROM MY SKETCHBOOK

My sons armed and serving the Lord: me behind in prayer.

God touching my hand as I cried out to Him for my son.

Jesus wrapping his arms around my three sons! Amen

Jesus meeting with my son Shane, comforting him.

Chapter 9

FOLLOWING GOD'S VOICE

"My sheep hear my voice, and I know them and they follow me."(John 10:27, NKJV)

Prayer is communicating with God, hearing His voice, and following Him. Henri Nouwen says, "God is always speaking. He's always doing something. Prayer is to enter into that activity. Prayer in its most basic sense is just getting into an attitude of saying, 'Lord, what are you saying to me?' " (*Prayer Powerpoints,* 134) God is always speaking to us so we must learn His voice. When we hear Him we must then follow Him. However, there are other voices that are also always speaking to us and want us to follow them. They fight for our attention, and much of the time we follow them and not God. One reason we do this is because we do not know it is happening. We are basically unaware.

Two other voices will always fight for your attention, and they are hard to shut down. These are the voices of two of your enemies, and one of your enemies may surprise you. It is you! Your own voice is self-focused and stubborn. It is the "what about me" voice of your flesh. If the voice uses the words "me, myself, or I", beware—you are in enemy territory. The other voice comes from the devil, and it is a deceitful, luring, and deadly voice. Remember, it is deceitful so it sounds like a voice you want to listen to; it sounds kind and correct. It is NOT! It will sound something like this: "You can walk out; you don't deserve this," or "No one will notice and it is only a small amount," or "You are saved, God isn't expecting you to do anything." These lies will destroy your plan and purpose, and that is what the devil is after!

This enemy's most deceitful voice is to those in church. He says, "You are saved, you go to church, you believe Jesus died for your sins." "You don't have to read your Bible and die to yourself, you only have to believe about Jesus." "You don't literally have to give up your life for Him. You can keep your life just the way it is. Lukewarm is fine, it gets you into heaven." Recognize the devil's voice because he is trying to kill you. "The thief comes to steal, kill, and destroy [You!]" (John 10:10). He does not use a knife, a rifle, or a sword. He uses deceit and lies and comes in through a weakness; a weakness in you.

If you are a believer, the enemy is after your plan and purpose. You may be busy serving, but is it the plan that God has for *you*? God placed gifts in you to build up the Kingdom of God. Satan does not want you to find fulfillment in your purpose. This is because if you walk in your purpose, this may mean many coming to know Christ through you, or you encouraging or helping other Christians grow spiritually. Your purpose is connected to souls and expanding the Kingdom. There will be fruit if you are using your gifts; not other people's fruit, your fruit! Roberts Lairdon, author and strong preacher, writes about evaluating where you spend your time. He says that some people wonder why *others* are increasing the Kingdom and writes, "They're doing their own business with their own hands! They are not running around taking care of everybody else's business! If you're running around taking care of everyone else's world, it's no wonder your world never grows or increases! God will not judge you on what you did to help another person's work; God will judge you on how well you did the work He assigned to you." (*Greater, Wiser, Stronger,* 29) Recognize the voice of the deceiver; look and listen. Is he stealing your purpose? Are you fulfilled? Are you producing fruit that lasts? Jesus said, "I chose you and appointed you so that you might go and bear fruit—fruit that will last" (John 15:16).

One night, my two sons, Brian and Shane and I went to hear an evangelist, Tommy Holohan at a local church. At the end of his preaching, Pastor Holohan did an altar call for those who wanted to give their lives to Christ or recommit their life. Some people came forward, and then he said that others needed to come up front. "Now there is an angel on one of your shoulders saying, 'You need to go up.' There is the devil on your other shoulder saying, 'Don't do it!' " Brian had already been saved and baptized and growing in the Lord. Now I was praying with everything I had, that Shane would go forward. He was standing next to me, and I felt him move. I opened my eyes, and Shane had gone forward! He went up to recommit his life to the Lord. Brian and I were hugging each other as tears rolled down my face! That voice of the deceiver lost again! Satan, you can't have my children!

Learn to recognize God's voice. God's voice says: "...Believe in the Lord Jesus Christ [give yourself up to Him, take yourself out of your own keeping and entrust yourself into His keeping] and you will be saved..." (Acts 16:31, AMP). "Not everyone who says to me, "Lord, Lord," will enter the kingdom of heaven, but only the one who does the will of my Father who is in heaven" (Matt.7:21). "Whoever tries to keep his life will lose it, and whoever loses his life will preserve it" (Luke 17:33, NKJV). "But why do you call Me, 'Lord, Lord', and do not do the things which I say?" (Luke 6:46, NKJV). "...So then, because you are lukewarm, and neither cold nor hot, I will vomit you out of my mouth" (Rev. 3:16, NKJV). "But do you want to know, O foolish man, that faith without works is dead. ...Do you see that faith was working together with his [Abraham's] works, and by works faith was made perfect. ...For as the body without the spirit is dead, so faith without works is dead also" (James 2:20, 22, 26, NKJV). Real saving faith shows in your life! How is your witness to others and yourself? Does it show? Do you know for sure God will say to you "Welcome" on that last day? You can know for sure, and you need to have this certainty. These Scriptures are the voice of God. He says, "Today, if you hear His voice, do not harden your hearts" (Hebrews 3:15, NKJV). "Do not merely listen to the word, and so deceive yourselves. Do what it says" (James 1:22). This is the voice of God speaking.

UNCONVERTED BELIEVERS

In his new book, *Follow Me,* David Platt, pastor and author, begins with Chapter One, "The Unconverted Believers." He recognizes this attack of the enemy, deceiving those who think they are believers. They are believers to a certain extent; they believe but are not yet converted to followers. There has not yet been a life changing, born again experience with the breath of God. If the Holy Spirit has come to live in a person, there has to be a life change, not just a mind change. A deceived person will have a belief in their mind, but not in their heart: there is knowledge of Him, but they don't know God personally. There is enough belief to feel comfortable about the life they are living, but are they going to hear, "Depart from me, I never knew you!"

Personally, I may have been an unconverted believer at one time until I cried out to God, "If I don't have the kind of faith to come into heaven, do something!" I either had a poor witness even to myself, or I was unconverted. I could not exist in that gray area. I needed to be certain and know that I know that I know! God heard my cry and started changing me. Now I know! Praise God!

Charlie was an unconverted believer most of his Christian life until he said to Pastor Grant that day in his office, "I finally get it! I have been in church my whole life doing nothing." God moved my husband from a doctrinal knowledge of Him to an experience with Him. Charlie started changing soon after reading the book, *Driven by Eternity.* In his book, John Bevere said he wrote the book after he had a dream where he saw many deceived Christians, meeting the Lord on Judgment Day, being thrown into Hell. The study of this book was a wake up call to my husband's deceived heart! Charlie was resting his eternal future on an incomplete gospel, "Believe in the Lord Jesus Christ and you will be saved" (Acts 16:31). He read, "If just believing in His existence and that He's the Son of God is all that's required to be saved, then James [James 2:17-19] shows the demons will be saved because they believe. That is ludicrous! ...The evidence of our truly being saved by the grace of Jesus Christ is that we will have the lifestyle to prove it." (*Driven by Eternity,* p. 90-91) Take Heed!

The devil is after your *plan* and *purpose* even more than he is after you! Your *plan* and *purpose* is what God has specifically designed as "your part" in His plan. It is an important part; it is yours and you will not find fulfillment in anything else. You will always be searching for what is missing. Your personality, gifts, and what excites you is all about Kingdom building. It will involve other souls being saved. My husband did not recognize the voice of the enemy, and because Satan deceived him for so many years, his plan and purpose was buried with him. The enemy was about stealing, killing and destroying Charlie's purpose. My son Colin said that he thinks God had a great plan for Dad. I totally agree. He wanted to evangelize. Sixty people raised their hand at his funeral to accept Jesus into their lives. Some of them could have truly been born again and will bring others to heaven with them. With others, a seed was planted. Amen to that! But, God had given my husband so many gifts which the enemy stole.

Charlie had so much passion that when he got excited about something he gave it his all. However, from the time I met him until a couple of months before he went to heaven, his passion was misdirected to making himself rich. I remember a candy vending machine business he started. He got the machines placed in stores, but keeping maintenance on them was the problem. One day he got a call from one of the business owners who told my husband that he had to take the machine out of his store because there were ants climbing all over it.

Candy did not work, but that did not stop him. Next he tried chickens. He met a musician from Ecuador at a street market in our town. Charlie was a very friendly person, and Mario became his friend. We had his wife and daughter over to our house several times and even took Mario to a Fernando Ortega concert. Mario actually lived in Ecuador and came to the United States for a few months a year with his music company. In Ecuador, he had a chicken farm and he was expanding. It was very expensive to borrow money in Ecuador, so Charlie and I made an investment in the chicken business. The numbers were good, but our partner was not. We got one profit check and then none after that. Someday I may travel to Quito, Ecuador and visit my chicken farm.

In 2002, Charlie and Colin went on a father-son mission trip to Bolivia. During this trip, Colin said that his father was always going off from the group, talking to local people. When Charlie got back home, he told me we needed to buy a warehouse; he had a new money-making idea. We were going to get into an import business. I thought he went on a mission trip! I hoped for a great conversion experience and missions in his blood! Wrong!! I just got a stomach ache thinking about the huge amount of money we would have to borrow to buy a warehouse. They did get some great pictures of Bolivia, however!

I met Charlie in a multi-level marketing health and nutrition business. We got married and joined forces, but I could barely keep up with him. He had packages being mailed out everywhere to prospective distributors. Each day was a crisis while nearing the time the post office would close. We Rushed! We Hurried! I would have loved to partner with him in ministry. I would say to him, "I want to go on a mission trip." He said, "You can go." I wanted him to want to go with me; that was the point!

I saw the gifts God had placed in Charlie. If only he would have "taken up his cross daily", but his days had been wasted. The enemy won in stealing Charlie's plan and purpose because Charlie had an orphan spirit. He was not affirmed by his earthly father, and so he sought validation elsewhere. The devil used this weakness, and Charlie bought the lie that money and success would make him happy. This open door to the enemy began to steal more and more from my husband during the last few years of his life. The Bible says, "No one can serve two masters. Either you will hate the one and love the other or you will be devoted to the one and despise the other. You cannot serve both God and money" (Matt.6:24).

But God got the victory! He won Charlie for the Kingdom, and my husband learned that true happiness only comes from a relationship with his heavenly Father through faith in Jesus. Since Charlie could have been such a great Kingdom builder, why did God take him so early at age 56? He was just getting started! He had only been on his new Kingdom assignment for eighteen days. Perry Stone, an international evangelist and author, gives this explanation, "At times there will be no visible reason why events play out as they do. It has been suggested that since God knows the future, He can allow some to arrive in heaven at an earlier age to prevent them from experiencing future trouble that could cost them their eternal destiny." We have to trust that God is Sovereign and there are things that we will never know or be able to understand on this side of heaven. (*Opening the Gates of Heaven,* p.70-71)

Not all things are good, but God causes all things to work together for good for His eternal purposes, to them who love God. (Romans 8:28) So by reading Charlie's story and how the enemy's voice deceived my husband and stole his purpose, you may hear God's voice calling to you. "Be not deceived, the thief has come only to steal, kill, and destroy; I have come that you may have life, and have it to the full" (John 10:10). The full life is the life He has planned for you before you were born. It is walking in your purpose. God says He has a plan: "For I know the plans I have for you" (Jeremiah 29:11). The devil is angry and knows he is lost, forever. He cannot come against God directly, but our enemy knows he still has a chance to capture people and take part of God's heart, which is *us*, to hell with him. If the devil has lost you to God, the deceiver is after your purpose. Can you understand that the enemy has a scheme designed specifically against you? It is to steal God's purpose for your life! Can you get up from where you are, close the door to the devil, and follow the voice of God your Father? If you do, then Charlie's stolen purpose will work for good! It will work in you! His testimony will be a weapon used against the enemy! Take that, devil!!

Chapter 10

PRAY WITH OTHERS!

"Again, I tell you that if two of you on earth agree about anything you ask for, it will be done for you by my Father in heaven". Matt.18:19

How did Jesus spend his life? He spent it praying! The disciples only asked Jesus to teach them one thing, "Lord, teach us to pray" (Luke 11:1). That is because every time they found Him, He was praying. He said, "For I did not speak of my own accord, but the Father who sent me commanded me what to say and how to say it. ...So whatever I say is just what the Father has told me to say" (John 12:49,50b). Jesus was in constant communication with the Father. Prayer is intimacy with God. When Jesus was baptized, He was praying. "And as he was praying, heaven was opened" (Luke 3:21b). When He chose the disciples, "Jesus went out to a mountainside to pray, and spent the night praying to God" (Luke 6:12). Jesus "often withdrew to lonely places and prayed" (Luke 5:16). Jesus modeled prayer as the center of His life, and it should be the center of ours also. We need solitary prayer for ourselves to grow closer and more intimate with the Father and to hear from Him. We also need to pray with others.

Jesus prayed with others. ". . .He took along Peter, John, and James, and went up on the mountain to pray" (Luke 9:22, NASB). When Jesus was praying in the Garden He found the disciples sleeping and said, "Could you not watch with me one hour?" (Matt. 26:40, NKJV). Jesus said, "My house shall be called a house of prayer for all nations" (Mark 11:17, NKJV). He encourages us to pray with others because, "Where two or three are gathered in my Name, I am there in the midst of them" (Matt. 18:20, NKJV). Uniting with other Christians in prayer gives prayer *power* because Jesus is there. Two or more believers filled with the Holy Spirit and praying God's will means, "It will be done for them by my Father in heaven" (Matt.18:19, NKJV). One of the devil's strategies is to separate us for he knows what can stop him. However, ". . .Because Jesus lives forever, he has a permanent priesthood. Therefore he is able to save completely those who come to God through him, because he always lives to intercede for them" (Hebrews 7:24-25). Jesus is praying to the Father for us, permanently and continuously! He is still praying for us. . . right now! Amen!

One Saturday I attended a special seminar offered at our church in Wheaton. It was about teens and drugs. The father who spoke told how his son was delivered from this serious problem. After the session I went up to him and asked what he really felt was the most effective thing he did to help his son. I do not remember any other information he gave because I probably already tried it and failed. But, what I DO remember, I will never forget. He said, "I got 700 people to pray for my son!" That was a powerful statement to me, and he did not need to say anything else. I was on it! This father told me exactly what God needed me to hear.

Since that day, I found many more opportunities to pray with others. I still continue to pray with my very good friend and prayer partner, Brenda. We met when our children attended the same Christian grade school, and now those six children are out of college. We always end our phone conversations with praying for our families. Brenda said that her mother is a woman of prayer and told her, "God has an 800 number, so why not call Him!" God also blessed me with a wonderful godly neighbor, Kim, who I prayed with for about a year until she moved out of state. I met another widow at Grief Share who became a prayer warrior with me. Jackie and

I went down to the beach and walked and prayed for our families a couple times a week for over a year!

At first, praying with others was difficult for me so I started with a group of two. You can't get any smaller than that so if you feel the same way, you can start there too! "Do not despise these small beginnings, for the Lord rejoices to see the work begin..." (Zechariah 4:10, NLT). James Banks, in his book, *The Lost Art of Praying Together* says, "God is merciful and accepts our efforts no matter how steep the learning curve may be. He works with us where we are and will make a way." (p.75) If you want to learn how to pray, spend time with those who know how to pray. Prayer is not something that comes naturally to us and is kind of like learning a foreign language. The best way to learn a foreign language is to put yourself in the environment where that language is spoken. The same works for learning to pray.

We are not to believe in Jesus just for ourselves, but to proclaim Jesus to others. One very easy and accepted way to do this is to ask a person if you could pray for them or for their family. Prayer brings people to the throne of God Himself! Jesus said that, "Where two or three gather together in my name, there am I with them" (Matthew 18:20). That is a promise from Jesus! So go ask a friend if they would like Jesus to show up and when they say "Yes!", pray with them in Jesus' name.

I seized opportunities to pray for my sons. I joined a Moms In Touch weekly prayer group for college-age children. Another prayer group I found very supportive was held at my church and was called "Praying for Our Prodigals." This group met for over a year. I still find great encouragement in the book I purchased through this group titled, *40 Days to Freedom, Prayers and Proclamations to Call Your Backslidden Children Into Their Destiny,* by Lanora Van Arsdall.

Another way I prayed with others was through Christian television. Whenever a number would come up on the screen as a number to call for prayer, I would call it. After my one son was delivered from drugs and gave his life to the Lord, Jackie's daughter wanted and needed to know what I did. She had a similar crisis in her home. My friend, Jackie, told her I called every time a number would come up on the television for someone to pray with! In addition to this, I also e-mailed in prayer requests, snail-mailed prayer requests and filled out prayer requests at my church. Whenever there was an opportunity to pray with others, I took it!

One time I called a local Christian radio station for prayer. I prayed with a wonderful Christian woman who took down my address and sent me an article titled, "Praying Your Family Into Heaven!" by Pastor Billy Joe Daugherty. I have used this article for many years and have shared it with many others. What a wonderful help this has been for me; I have memorized and prayed these Scriptures so often for my family and others. I have no idea how many workmen I have prayed to come across my sons' paths, perhaps hundreds! (Matt 9:38)

At my Sunday School Class, we were asked if we had any prayer requests we wanted prayed for in class. This is in addition to the written prayer requests. Two of the prayers I asked our class to pray for, God heard and answered in a mighty way! One was a miracle for my son! The other was for a teenage girl in my neighborhood. She told me she had not had a friend since she moved here in fourth grade. I asked for prayers that God would give her a Christian friend. Soon after that, she shared with me about her *new* friend who she was attending youth group with at my church. Over the last few years I have seen her grow so much in her faith. She has a passion for the Lord and His Word, and she has so much joy! God does amazing things when we pray with others. Our Class has some powerful prayer warriors! How encouraging!

MY VERY SPECIAL PRAYER PARTNER

After my husband's baptism, I realized I now had a prayer partner. This was very exciting, and I felt relieved. I was not the lone warrior anymore! I could pray with him for our three sons to be saved; I had reinforcement. It was comforting to know that Charlie was standing in the battle along side me. I felt like I had just returned from fighting a major war praying for him, but God had given me the victory! I now knew prayer worked. I remember asking Charlie to pray with me, and that God would please save one of our sons. He gave me the strangest look like, "Why would you ask that?", and said, "I don't want just one of them saved, I want all of them saved!"

We prayed together that God would save all three of our sons. The prayers we pray continue on; they do not disappear. That one prayer Charlie prayed with me for our sons is still alive. I treasure what E.M. Bounds writes in his book, "Prayers are deathless. The lips that uttered them may be closed in death, the heart that felt them may have ceased to beat, but the prayers live before God, and God's heart is set on them and prayers outlive the lives of those who uttered them: outlive a generation, outlive an age, outlive a world." (*Understanding Prayer,* p.8) Now, I cannot believe I was serious about "one" son; that God would not save them all! The reason I thought about asking God to save one son, was because of how much it took to pray for Charlie. He had no idea! Could God really give me more than one miracle? I had a whole lot more to learn about prayer and a whole lot more to learn about God.

I am thankful that Charlie had great faith and a fresh anointing, being recently saved by the blood of Jesus. He had the right prayer according to God's will, "not wanting anyone to perish, but everyone to come to repentance" (2 Peter 3:9).

God will do it! "If two of you agree here on earth, concerning anything you ask, my Father in heaven will do it for you" (Matt.18:19, NLT). Thankfully, Charlie was still here on earth just long enough for both of us to be able to agree in prayer for our three sons! Now, how special was that prayer? It was a miracle in itself!

Chapter 11

CRY OUT!

"Have mercy on me Lord, for I call to you all day long!"
Psalm 86:3

I had been praying for the four men in my family for what seemed like forever. Nothing ever seemed to change. Was God hearing anything I was saying? One night, after my husband had moved full-time down to Florida, he said something to me which just hurt! I cannot remember anything about what he said, but I do remember saying to myself, "How many times do I forgive? Was it really seventy times seven?" When Peter asked Jesus, how many times was he to forgive, Jesus said, "I tell you, not seven times, but seventy-seven times" (Matt.18:22). I felt that I was surely on 78 by Now! I just had to leave and go outside to get away. It was a dark, quiet night, and I was emotionally exhausted as I walked around our neighborhood. With tears running down my face, I cried out to God, "Lord, please have mercy on me! When are You EVER, going to answer one of my prayers?" I remember saying that word, "ever" with such desperation that I may have compelled God to move. I truly think that on this night, I touched God's heart.

Over the next couple months, my husband started changing. I could see God answering my prayers for my husband. God did have mercy on me and performed a miracle! He says that "in the day of trouble", if I call upon Him, He promises to answer. "In the day of my trouble, I will call upon You, for You will answer me" (Psalm 86:7, NKJV). He did answer me! I had been praying earnestly for my husband for over five years, but this is the first time I remember crying out from the bottom of my soul! I was desperate for God's mercy. I think that "the day of trouble" is the day that you are holding on by a thread. In desperation, you cry out for Him. It is unlike any other prayer; it is desperate! God knows that you know He is the only One who can help. It was the end of me and the beginning of "God, now it is only You". Within three months I had not only an answer to prayer... but a MIRACLE! Charlie was born again and baptized! Before he went under the water at his Baptism, he said, "I would like to apologize to my wife, to my family and to God!" Why now and so quickly? Perhaps because of my desperate cry, "Lord, have mercy on me!"

God gave me a wonderful neighbor friend for a season. She was a strong Christian woman who had a heart for God and who loved to pray. She would come over to my house, and we would pray together for our children almost daily for months. She and her family had to move back to Colorado due to personal reasons. Before she moved, she gave me her book, *The Power of Crying Out, When Prayer Becomes Mighty*, by Bill Gothard. One thing I read in his book verified that night I called out to God. Bill Gothard says, "I saw that the Bible makes a distinction between "prayer" and "crying out to God." ...He will arrange or allow circumstances to arise that seem to have no solution—and then do nothing to remove the problem. Until I cry out. And not one second sooner!" (p.12)

Sometimes it seems like we wait so long for God to answer us but then, all of a sudden, God moves... and moves quickly! Why does He wait? Perhaps He is waiting for us. He is waiting for: our lives to line up with His will, our faith to grow, our prayers to become more fervent, His glory to be magnified, our obedience to the Word and us to cry out. Jeremiah 33:3 tells us to call, "Call to Me, and I will answer you, and show you great and mighty things, which you do not know" (NASB). In Psalm 34:15 we read that God hears our cry. "The eyes of the Lord are on the righteous, and His ears are open to their cry" (NKJV). Jonah also cried out. "In my distress I called to the Lord, and he answered me. From the depths of the grave I called for help, and you listened to my cry" (Jonah 2:2). Peter too, became afraid and cried out, "When he saw the wind, he was afraid and, beginning to sink, cried out, Lord save me! Immediately Jesus reached out his hand and caught him" (Matt. 14:30-31a). *Immediately*! Jesus is so close to us; He can just reach out. Why isn't He? Are you desperate for His hand? Maybe He needs your voice and heart to *cry out*!

Chapter 12

PROCLAIM YOUR LIFE VERSE!

"...I will even make a road in the wilderness, and rivers in the desert." Isaiah 43:19b (NKJV)

It was May 9, 2007, around noon. Charlie and I were driving home from an appointment we had with a wonderful real estate broker who I was planning to start working for. Charlie was going to help me with the new technology she used, and he and I were going back the next day for training. We were under heavy financial pressure, and I was not enthusiastic but willing to help. I had success at selling real estate in the past and had studied and passed the test in Florida. I was stepping up to the plate!

On this ride home, I pulled out a small prayer booklet I was carrying called, *The Prayer that Changes Everything*, by Stormie Omartian. I prayed this prayer with my husband, and it was the last prayer we prayed together. It was titled, "When I Seek Breakthrough, Deliverance, or Transformation."

> Heavenly Father, thank You that You have delivered me out of the enemy's hand. I know You will continue to deliver me until the day I go to be with You. I call upon Your name, Lord. " I implore You, deliver my soul." (Psalm 116:4) I know You have begun a good work in me and You will complete it. (Phil. 1:6) I know that in what ever state I am, I can be content because You will not leave me there forever. (Phil. 4:11) [I said, "Charlie, He will not leave us here forever."] I will praise You in the midst of any

need I have for breakthrough, deliverance, or transformation, knowing that You see my need and will meet it in Your way and in Your time. (Omartian, p. 104)

Then I read the verse that went with this prayer. It became my life verse. *Do not remember the former things, nor consider the things of old. Behold I will do a new thing, now it shall spring forth; shall you not know it? I will even make a road in the wilderness and rivers in the desert* (Isaiah 43:18-19, NKJV).

That night Charlie died of a heart attack. God did not leave him there forever, as we had just prayed in that final prayer, but brought him to heaven where Charlie was totally transformed. God says, "Dear friends, now we are children of God, and what we will be has not yet been made known. But we know that when Christ appears, we shall be like him, for we shall see him as he is" (1 John 3:2). As Christians, we are being sanctified, becoming more and more like Christ, as we renew our minds with the Word. However, when we get to heaven and see Jesus face-to-face, the process is complete, and we "shall be like Him." Charlie is like Christ!

Since then, this verse has become my life verse. It says that in the past, the miracles were nothing compared to what God would do in the future. God did a miracle in delivering the Israelites and parting the Red Sea. He says to forget that, because in this new wilderness, "I will do new and better miracles for my people." The miracle of Charlie being born again and rescued just in time, will not compare to the miracles which lie ahead for me. I needed this hope! In this new wilderness, my life as a widow, I wanted to stay strong for my sons and stay in prayer for them. They also needed miracles. It has been almost six years since that day, and I have prayed out loud many times, "Lord, You will make a road in the wilderness. You will do it. I believe You and trust You!" This verse gives me His peace, knowing that God will do what He has promised. I meditate on and have memorized this Scripture. In times when I felt lost, the Holy Spirit comforted me by reminding me of this verse. He says, "Hold on to this! *I am* doing a new thing. *I am* making a way!"

When you are reading the Word and a verse jumps out at you and speaks to you and your spirit comes alive, this is God talking to you. This is how God uses Scripture. Graham Cooke, Christian author and speaker, calls this your "Inheritance verse." He says, "God loves to open up Scripture and choose the passage that He wants you to live in! Now! . . . He is giving you a promise for your life. He was giving you your Inheritance word. When God gives *you* a passage of Scripture, what He is saying to you, everything in this passage belongs to You. . .every experience, every encounter in that passage, *you* are meant to have those experiences and those encounters!" (*The Art of Thinking Brilliantly,* CD-ROM) I am experiencing this to be true!

I have four other "Inheritance verses" God has given me. One is "All your sons will be taught by the Lord, and great will be your children's peace" (Isaiah 54:13). The second one is, "The seed of the righteous shall be delivered" (Proverbs 11:21b, KJV). I have these two verses taped to my mirror so I can be reminded of them every day. Many days I proclaim them out loud, knowing that God watches over His Word to perform it.

A third verse is, "Be still and know that I am God" (Psalm 46:10, NKJV). I cannot tell you how many times I have had to trust in the Lord with this verse over the past six years. I would say it has been my "go to" verse. Many times I have had great concern for my sons having to handle their grief, anger, depression and even staying alive due to drug use! God would speak to me and remind me that He is God, He knows all, can do all, and has all things under control. I have this verse on a stone tile in my kitchen and have stood in my kitchen many times staring at this tile hanging onto His Word. One Christmas, my neighbor gave me a cross with this verse on it. She was so excited to give me this because she knew it was "my verse." I would meditate on it until I received the peace of God.

My other "Inheritance verse" is Ecclesiastes 3:11, "God has made everything beautiful in its time." God just wants me to know this and remember this. He will make all things just beautiful! It is going to be great! Be patient, it takes time. Keep going. I have a magnet on my refrigerator with this special verse. Sometimes I move it to my desk so I can see it while I am at my computer. What a great thought! What a kind God to give me that special verse! I think of it as God giving me this huge promise of Hope.

The key to believing these words in these promises is knowing God's voice. Having the knowledge of the words does not bring power, but knowing the One who gave the words does. The relationship with God and the work (power) of the Holy Spirit brings life to the promises. According to Andrew Murray, "The presence of God Himself as the Promiser, not the knowledge of what He has promised, awakens faith and trust in prayer." (*With Christ in the School of Prayer,* p.164) So true!

Besides these verses, I just have verses! I have verses taped to my bathroom wall, my mirror, my desk, on hundreds of note cards, on magnets, and most importantly, many in my heart. It is raining verses, showering promises, grace falling and God whispering throughout my home! I love Bible verses. I wonder if the room He is preparing for me has Bible verses etched all over my walls in gold! Could be!

Chapter 13

PERSEVERE!

"Men always ought to pray and do not lose heart."
(*Luke* 18:1, NKJV)

Three Thankful Hearts

It was Mother's Day, May 13, 2007, and the day of my husband's wake. I was at the funeral home back in our hometown of Wheaton, Ill. and it was nearing 3 o'clock. The doors would soon open for friends and family to come in and pay their last respects and give their condolences. The funeral director came up to me and said that some more flowers had arrived and wanted me to see them before he opened the doors.

I walked into the room with my husband's casket and in Charlie's arms lay a bouquet of red roses. My wonderful and amazing sons bought these, along with the most treasured Mother's Day card I had ever received. It was from Charlie! It said, **"For my Wife with Love"** on the front, followed by three messages on the inside written to me, one by each son. They wrote as if Charlie was speaking to me, but each of their hearts had the same "Thank you, Mom, message." The most significant part of what they each wrote was:

"...You have always been the spiritual leader of our family and without you we wouldn't have been what we are today. You were always a sweetheart to me and the boys and I love that." (Brian)

"...Thanks for never giving up on me...You were right! Most importantly, thanks for being a living example of a strong Christian woman and servant to myself and our boys. Without that leadership (yours), our family would have fallen apart, but your devotion to God and our family kept us together. Thank You! Forever and Ever!" (Colin)

". . . I am honored to have such a wife as you. You are a great example to me with your never-dying faith. This has shown me how I should live my life. Without you and your persistence, I would have still been wandering around lost in this world. Like I said at my baptism, I am sorry to you and the boys for being so selfish. Because of you and my new heart for the Lord, we can be great examples for our sons....Stay strong in your faith, pray with the kids, and spend time with them. Until you get here, I will be doing my new gardening job! See you soon, Love, Your husband, Charlie." (Shane)

First of all, you will have to read John Bevere's book, *Rescued*, to understand what Shane was saying about Charlie's new gardening job! I recommend that you do. Secondly, after reading these touching words from my sons' hearts, I was already in tears, and the doors were about to open! How totally blessed I was to have sons who thought of their mother, and reached out in such a loving way to comfort me! All four of us were grieving, but all four of us were thankful to God, that we knew that their Dad, my husband, was safe with God. He was an eleventh hour man. Charlie was outside the Kingdom until the very last days of his life, but the Lord still calls at the eleventh hour. (Matt. 20:6, KJV) This was how God comforted us, and this was a miracle! "Lord, I praise You because you are the God who performs miracles; you display your power among the peoples" (Psalm 77:14). Thirdly, I could see that God was already working in my sons' hearts, seeing what was truly important in life, and that only what we do for Christ will matter for eternity. "Why you do not even know what will happen tomorrow. What is your life? You are a mist that appears for a little while and then vanishes" (James 4:14). And also, "For we must all appear before the judgment seat of Christ, that each one may receive the things done in the body, according to what he has done, whether good or bad" (2Cor. 5:10, KJV).

He Will Do It

God promises rewards to those who seek Him as we read in Hebrews 11:6, "He that cometh to God must believe that he is, and that he is a rewarder of them who diligently seek Him" (KJV). The key is diligence and persistence. I was pursuing God for the lives of my husband and sons. God rewarded me with my husband saved and safe in heaven; the miracle I never quit praying for. The "I never quit praying" was also all about God. I just kept moving as *He* put the book in my hand, the church in my path, the sermon I needed to hear, the friend to encourage me, a Scripture to strengthen me and the Holy Spirit to guide me. God says, "The one who calls you is faithful and He will do it!" (1 Thes.5:24). As long as I continued seeking Him in prayer, God was working behind the scenes on His miracle, Charlie!

It is amazing how God worked in our family, and He started with me. Jentzen Fanklin, pastor and author, says that God puts a diamond in a family, which is the first one to come to Christ. He says, "I believe God hovers over families and He finds one single, solitary diamond in every family. He sovereignly picks one member of the family to deliver those bound with spiritual chains." *(Right People, Right Place, Right Plan, p..190)* One is a majority partnered with God! Psalm 68:6 says, "God setteth the solitary in families: he bringeth out those which are bound with chains" (KJV). If God can get one in a family, He can free the rest. I truly believe that God put me in this family for this time, to reach the rest of my family for Christ. This was a big assignment that was going to take Navy Seal spiritual growth training, but the Holy Spirit was the perfect drill sergeant. I was here "for such a time as this" and if I remained silent, my family could perish! (Esther 4:14). If I did my part—pray, I was confident that God would do His part. "With man, this was impossible, but with God all things are possible" (Matt. 19:26).

I also believe that God has put a great plan and purpose in each one of my sons' lives, and that is why the enemy has fought so hard to destroy them. He was relentless, but so was I! God already won, but I had to stay on the battlefield! Retreat was not an option. Jentzen Franklin also says that, "When you ask God for a miracle, He will often give you a set of instructions—a plan." Joshua's instructions to conquer a city, involved marching around the walls of Jericho for seven days and then blowing horns. Naaman was to wash in the Jordan River seven times to be healed of leprosy. (*Right People, Right Place, Right Plan,* p.104-105) I asked God for a miracle for my family: My first instruction was "Move," the second was "Learn to pray" and the third was "Don't quit!"

Violent Faith

When I relocated to Florida, I developed a case of "violent faith!" I was at war with the enemy for my family. Judy Jacobs, dynamic speaker, minister and author, says, "Violent faith is active. It is constantly changing and moving according to the tide of the Spirit for a particular time, situation, or circumstance." She says it looks like Abraham ready to bring the knife down on Isaac, his son. It looks like Esther saying, "If I perish, I perish." and it looks like Jacob wrestling with the angel saying, "I will not let you go until you bless me." (Gen.22:11, Esther 4:16, Gen. 3:26) (*Stand Strong,* p.141) This was me: Abraham, Esther, and Jacob. I have lived in all these stories.

Like Abraham, I remember having a vision of me putting my son, Brian, on the Altar. I finally came to realize that I could not go around the mountain the same way one more time! I feared that he would end up in some back yard, dead from an overdose, but what I was doing was not helping. I stopped trying to help, and I released him to God. At that point I sowed my faith as a seed, and then God was able to provide a harvest. Brian said that this was the turning point for him. At another time, I pictured myself as Esther. I stood up and went forward into enemy territory warring for my son, Colin. Satan was not going to have my son. If I perished, I perished! And, like Jacob, I was not letting go until I saw the victory! With both these sons, I remember a point of release to God, and it was then that God provided. One powerful prayer is the prayer of release; letting go and putting everything in God's hands.

The night my husband died, I felt like I was in a Bible story. It was as if I fought Goliath! God put that stone right in the enemy's forehead by Charlie giving his life to Christ. Now it was time for Charlie to come home. The story was so supernatural, I saw it as God's story. The battle was over, and God won. Sitting on the sofa alone that night, I felt God's presence all around me. However, I was totally blindsided by how this story took a dramatic turn. I dug deep down to a new level of trust in God, and now more than ever....I clung onto Him. At first, I would often wake up feeling as if I was falling out of an airplane! I held onto God for me and my three sons; I needed His strength and they needed mine. The war was not over, I was still on the battlefield. But now, because of God's miracle, my husband secure with Him in eternity, I knew God heard me, and He was right there with me. "Never will I leave you. Never will I forsake you" (Hebrews 13:5b). My faith rested in Him. What He did was perfect and best. . . no matter how difficult. As the Word says, "My thoughts are not your thoughts, neither are your ways my ways," declares the Lord. "As the heavens are higher than the earth, so are my ways higher than your ways and my thoughts than your thoughts" (Isaiah 55:8-9). I believed God! I never asked why.

"Get Up, Suit Up, We are Going In!"

Those next months were emotionally exhausting and physically draining. The enemy was not happy that he lost the war for my husband's soul, and he seemed to be out for revenge. He now knew my name. (Acts 19:15) Besides legal work, business responsibilities, moving, helping sons with college admission issues, there were emotions to work through. My son in Chicago was hurting very deeply. In Florida, I was seeking God for a breakthrough with my son Brian whose life was spiraling out of control. I was trying to maintain some stability for my other son, Shane, who was preparing to start his first year away at college. God was my only source, and prayer was my only weapon—but it was nuclear! I felt one of us, Brian or myself, was not going to live through the summer, and it was a very low point for me. The devil was trying to wear me down, wanting me to give up my fight, and he was coming close to winning. God says to, "Stay alert. Watch out for your great enemy, the devil. He prowls around like a roaring lion, looking for someone to devour" (1Pet.5:8, NLT). I was on his menu.

I still remember the night God picked me up and gave me the strength to press on. It was a month and a half after Charlie's death and Pastor Grant who officiated my husband's funeral, was speaking in our large sanctuary at church. It was a Wednesday night, and I definitely wanted to go and hear him. The enemy tried to prevent this from happening; he set up a barricade. What Satan does is not an accident. I had a huge conflict with Brian, and all I remember is that it was drug related. I was exhausted, but somehow, God made sure I got to the church. I was very late, and so I sat down in the back of the church. I was able to listen to about a fourth of

Pastor Grant's sermon; the part God wanted me to hear; the part that inspired me to persevere in praying for the next miracle! Satan is not threatened by more knowledge or activity; but prayer he needs to stop! God said to me, "Get up, suit up, we are going in!"

I started listening and could not believe what I heard. The last part of the sermon was about Charlie and me! God made sure I was there to hear this. Pastor Grant was on part four of his sermon and it was titled, "Pray and Persevere." He told my husband's story, and how I never became offended enough to ever stop praying for him. Even though Charlie and the boys said to "Lay off, we are doing fine the way we are," Judy never gave up and surrounded herself with friends to help pray them through. He talked about Charlie's funeral and how sixty people raised their hand to accept Jesus. Pastor Grant asked,

> "What if Judy would have stopped praying? What if she stopped the day before Charlie died? Sixty people would not have been saved and Charlie may not have made heaven. You talk about the power of a praying wife. I know they put her through a lot of stuff. I know it wasn't easy for her. But the confirmation to prayers answered, she persevered time and time again. You need to work the plan God gave you. Don't allow the devil to rub out one more day of your life. Don't stop praying. I know it was tough for her, but talk about a persevering person." ("Offenses Will Come". First Assembly of God, Fort Myers, Fl. June 24, 2007, Sermon.)

My eyes were wide open, and I was on the edge of my seat! God was showing me that my prayers matter, and they make an eternal difference. Pastor Grant talked about Joseph not giving up, David not giving up and *me* not giving up. God was drawing me close and talking right to me! I wanted to persevere like Judy! My story helped *me*! It was as if God brought me here, sat down next to me and said, "Listen to this!" "For I am the Lord, your God, who takes hold of your right hand and says to you. . . Do not fear, I will help you!" (Isaiah 41:13)

Then Pastor ended with asking those to stand up if they were struggling, right now, where God has you. That if you have been praying for a husband or a family member and you are growing weary, you need to stand right now! I stood right up!! He then prayed for God to give us the perseverance to continue to pray for our loved ones and to empower us with His strength. He prayed that God would do a supernatural work in our child or spouse, and that His plan be revealed in their lives. He prayed that we would have hope that things would change, and that we would be patient for the plan that He has for our lives. Finally, that we would pray and persevere for others, that the weight would come off and we would be rejuvenated in God's strength, because God was in control.

I felt the power of God strengthen me in my spirit and give me a second wind! It was God saying to me, "Be strong and courageous. Do not be afraid or discouraged. For the Lord your God is with you wherever you go" (Joshua 1:9). I left the church ready to persevere in prayer and work the plan that God had for me. I had three sons whose lives needed God's intervention. I returned to the battlefield that night. The Lord had frustrated the enemy's attack on me. I was ready to follow orders, "Don't be afraid of them. Remember the Lord, who is great and awesome, and fight for your brothers, your sons and your daughters, your wives and your homes" (Ne. 4:14).

In Revelation 12:11 we read, "They overcame him by the Blood of the Lamb and the word of their testimony, and they did not love their lives to the death" (NKJV). This is what God did for me that night. I won the war with the enemy trying to defeat me. First, by knowing who I was in Christ and that He was with me. Secondly, through the testimony of what He had already done! "Judy, I already have one miracle. What I did once, I will do again." I needed to be reminded of my history with God so I could go into this next battle. Joshua placed a memorial of 12 stones at Gilgal to be a constant reminder of how God dried up the Jordan River so the Israelites could cross. "He did this so all the nations of the earth might know that the Lord's hand is powerful. . ." (Joshua 4:24). I, God's frontline prayer warrior, needed a reminder that the Lord's powerful hand was with me. Like David, who looked back at his past victories with God, killing the lion and the bear (1 Sam 17:37), I needed to look back at Charlie's victory with God. David gained courage to fight Goliath, and I gained courage to fight my next Goliath, a son addicted to drugs. I broke the intimidation Satan was trying to put on me by "not loving my life to the death" (Rev 12:11b). I cared more about what God wanted me to do and the love for my sons, than what it was going to take for me to stay strong in prayer.

This was going to be one, fierce battle! I needed to learn what was in my arsenal. God impressed on me, "For though we walk in the flesh, we do not war after the flesh: For the weapons of our war-fare are not carnal, but mighty through God to the pulling down of strongholds" (2 Cor.10:3-4, KJV). God also reminded me about my mission: "Pray for the four men in my family—for them to know ME." The Word says, "You did not choose me, but I chose you and appointed you that you should go and bear fruit—fruit that will last" (John15:16a). He also said to finish my assignment. Quitting is not an option. "See to it that you complete the ministry that you received in the Lord" (Col. 4:17). God gave me *our* war strategy: press into Me with all your heart, listen to the Holy Spirit for orders and persevere in prayer. "We're movin' out!!"

Discovering More Weapons

I felt I needed help so I called my church to see if counseling was available. It was not, but I *was* able to spend some time talking with a kind woman who suggested that I "fast." That sounded like a mighty weapon. I learned that we are to fast in obedience to the Word and for breakthrough. In the Bible, Jesus fasted and prayed. He expects us to fast and pray. When we do, we should not let others notice. There are many examples of fasting in the Old Testament and the New Testament. The sixth chapter of Matthew is about seeking God first. We read, "Seek first his kingdom and his righteousness and all these things will be given to you as well" (Matt.6:33). Fasting is about putting God first and is talked about in this same chapter. Matt.6:16,18 says, "And when you fast, don't make it obvious. . . And your Father, who sees everything, will reward you" (NLT).

Obedience to fasting draws you closer to God and produces great spiritual results and breakthroughs. You must die to your flesh which gives strength to your spirit. It will make your prayers more powerful and break the yoke of bondage. It shows your dependency on God. It empowers you and it gives you spiritual strength. Queen Esther was going to put her life on the line for her people and so she called a fast; asking for prayer to God for His STRENGTH! "Go and gather together all the Jews who are in Susa and fast for me....When this is done, I will go to see the king, even though it is against the law. If I perish, I perish" (Esther 4:16). Andrew Murray says, "Fasting helps to express, to deepen, and to confirm the resolution that we are ready to sacrifice anything, even ourselves, to attain the Kingdom of God." (*With Christ In the School of Prayer,* p.101) My son's situation was a life and death matter! I needed to sacrifice for him. I added fasting to my persevering prayers. Holy Spirit orders!

I added yet another weapon to my arsenal. I learned about praying in the Spirit. When I attended a conference at our church, I received the baptism of the Holy Spirit. All I knew was that if God was offering more, and it was biblical and available, I needed it and wanted it. Tim Enloe, speaker and author, explained the five encounters we have with the Holy Spirit. He **convicts** us of our sin and need for God, **regenerates** us at the time we are born again, **indwells** in us at the moment we are born again, **matures** us as Christians and **empowers** us. This final experience with the Holy Spirit empowerment is an anointing for the power to minister, to share our faith and for miracles. (*Want More?*, p.24) Jesus said, "You will receive power when the Holy Spirit comes upon you. And you will be my witnesses, telling people about me everywhere" (Acts 1:8, NLT). There are two kinds of intercessory prayer available, and now I was able to use both! One was from my understanding and one from God's. The Bible says, ". . . the Spirit helps us in our weakness. We do not know what we ought to pray for, but the Spirit himself intercedes for us with groans that words cannot express. . .the Spirit intercedes for the saints in accordance with God's will" (Romans 8:26-27). Many times I did not even know what to pray, but God did.

Most Surely!

When your husband dies, you become a widow! This was a difficult step for me—to accept this new title. The first time I had to fill out a form and check that box, it was hard. However, it drew me to the parable in the Bible of the persistent widow. I liked that, it was me! I prayed daily for the salvation and deliverance of my sons and continually kept my requests before Him throughout the day. I kept believing and having faith no matter what things looked like in the natural. Jesus told this parable to show that we should not give up in prayer and how the widow kept going back to the *unjust* judge. This judge finally gave her justice. Jesus wants us to do the same, but also said, "So don't you think God will surely give justice to his chosen people who cry out to him day and night? Will he keep putting them off?" (Luke 18:7b, NLT). In contrast, God is *just*, *loving* and *good*. So "surely", He was promising me that with patient, persistent, persevering prayer accompanied by great faith, the answer was on its way.

It took great faith to make it through that year. There were seven years of prayer for Brian before I, like Elijah, saw "a cloud as small as a man's hand." Elijah sent his servant back seven times to look for rain. Each time the servant returned and reported nothing, but Elijah continued to pray, was not discouraged and did not give up because God gave him a promise. (1Kings 18:44) My "small cloud" was a text message I received from Brian, "I need to see a doctor." I had great faith to not give up, but unlike Elijah, I did get discouraged. God had to keep picking me up and putting me back on the battlefield. He used His Word to encourage me. "Keep on asking, and you will receive what you ask for. Keep on seeking, and you will find. Keep on knocking, and the door will be opened to you!" (Matt. 7:7, NLT). Also, Luke 1:37 says, "With God nothing shall be impossible." This was impossible for me, but only with God as I kept asking, seeking, and knocking would the miracle "surely" come.

One of the "I see nothing" nights, I was on my knees praying that Brian would return home safely. At church that week, we heard devastating news of a granddaughter found dead in a backyard of a bad neighborhood. She died from a cocaine overdose. I relied on another Bible story to make it through those long hours. A vast army was coming against Judah and Jehoshaphat. They sought God in prayer because He was the only one who could save the nation. God said, "Do not be afraid or discouraged because of this vast army. For the battle is not yours, but God's.... You do not have to fight in this battle. Take up your positions, stand firm and see the deliverance the Lord will give you..." (2Ch.20:15, 17). I took my stand before the Lord, *on my knees*! I clung to "Be still and know that I am God" (Psalm 46:10). I remained on my knees and prayed until Brian returned home.

God fought and won the battle that night and many battles after that! *Eventually*, God won the war against the enemy for Brian's soul. Brian became a child of God for the Glory of God! This added to my history with God; another Goliath defeated and another miracle! Now I was ***truly believing*** in the God I believed in! If you do what God says to do, He promises He will **surely** do what He says He will do.

He Will Strengthen You

By January of 2012, God had blessed me with two miracles; my eleventh hour husband, Charlie, and my son, Brian ... saved, delivered and serving the Lord. However, I had another huge mountain that I wanted cast into the sea. My son Colin needed so much prayer. He also needed a miracle. I had been praying for him for seven years, too! However, there was a problem. I was tired and emotionally weak. The enemy must have known that he was in danger of losing again, so he wanted to steal my fight. I recognized signs in myself that I was spiraling down emotionally. Perhaps, I was feeling the weight of my son's pain. But God had prepared me ahead of time for this, and I took action. The Word says, "Submit to God, resist the devil, and he will flee from you" (James 4:7, NKJV). The key is submitting to God. I knew I needed *His* strength and so I wrote verses on note cards about *His* strength. I started meditating on them and praying them. Psalm 105:4 says, "Seek the Lord and his strength, and seek his face evermore" (NKJV). Isaiah 41:10 reads, "Fear not, for I am with you; do not be dismayed, for I am your God; I will strengthen you, I will help you, I will uphold you with my righteous right hand." I kept praying for strength and God was faithful again! I felt a shift in my spirit! I felt **His Strength**!

After praying to God for weeks, I remember sitting in my den on that burgundy leather chair seeking Him, when the power of God came over me. The Holy Spirit strengthened my spirit, and He stood me right up! I said, "God, if you have called me to do this, I will do it." I felt my fight back and my authority returned. I had another "Esther" moment with my King, "for such a time as this, You have called me to fight for my son." It was amazing what God did; He gave me my third wind! Again He said, "Get up, suit up, we're going in!" 2Tim. 4:5b says to "Fully carry out the ministry God has given you" (NLT). This means to do all that it entails and complete it with all that it takes because it was given to you by God. No one else had been assigned to pray for the four men in my family. Only I could do this ministry given to *me*. God says once more, "For I am the Lord, your God, who takes hold of your right hand and says to you, Do not fear; I will help you!"(Isa. 41:13).

Back on prayer duty and seeking the Lord for my son, within a few weeks Colin said he gave his life to the Lord! Within three months he had gone into full-time ministry, joining his brother. The enemy knew God was close to victory and wanted to make a last effort to stop the rescue. One of his last tactics was to try and take out this "praying mother." On my refrigerator I keep a little saying from David Jeremiah which says, "No child is more fortunate than one with a praying parent or grandparent." This is so true, because these are the ones who will not give up, will do whatever it takes and will persist and persevere for the souls of their children. This is the only place these heartfelt, fervent prayers can come from. This deep love overlooks rejection, anger, hurt and rebellion, and does not stop praying until it sees the miracle. Seeing my vision of Jesus wrapping his arms around my sons and knowing He has a great purpose to be fulfilled by them, keeps me bringing my prayers to the Father who loves them more than me. And that is a **Halleluiah!**

Chapter 14

PRAY GOD'S WILL!

"...If we ask anything, according to his will, he hears us."
1 John 5:14

      One Sunday after the church service, I went up to my pastor with a concern for my son. He was engaged, but that was the concern. They had been dating for seven years, and I had been praying about this situation all those years. I prayed for his salvation, her salvation and for her whole family. There were also many, many other issues including extreme co-dependency, control and much dysfunction. Whenever I would talk with my son about this, about waiting on the Lord, he would not speak to me for months. These were very, very difficult times. He got angry, and I just hurt. They began making plans for the wedding, even though I could not see how my son was in any way healthy enough to get married. He had decided to quit his very stressful job and was becoming very depressed. I asked the Lord ahead of time to help me get through that wedding day. When I talked to my son on the phone, I felt much concern for his emotional and mental state. I devoted myself to persistent and fervent prayer for him. I called prayer ministers to pray with me over the phone. At Sunday school, when they asked for prayer concerns, I just asked that they please pray for a miracle and that God would touch his life.

      When I went up front to speak to my pastor that day, I explained to him that I did not know how to pray anymore for my son. Do I pray that they would break up, that both would come to know the Lord, or what? I had been praying for seven years and the situation was getting worse. He said very simply,

"Just pray God's will." That is what I started to do again for him. I felt HOPE! It just gave me better direction and confidence. I prayed that my son would come to know Jesus as his Lord and Savior and that God would heal, protect and deliver him. I also prayed, "Lord, Your will be done in his relationship." I now pray for God's will at the end of all my prayers. "Your Kingdom come, Your will be done" (Matt. 6:10).

During this same time, Colin's brother, Brian, reminded me that he was also praying for him. Brian said he even prayed with others for Colin. Together we had powerful, heartfelt prayers coming from the East coast and the West coast! I later found out that my three sisters were also praying for their nephew, Colin. They had recently seen him at another nephew's wedding reception and were very concerned for him. I like to think that our prayers met in heaven and together they moved the hand of God! Within a month, my son gave his life to the Lord! Within four months God delivered him instantly from a serious addiction as others prayed over him! A week later, he broke off his engagement and went full-time into ministry! God performed another miracle! I could hardly believe it! Really? Thank You, Lord! To You I give all the honor and praise and glory! After all those years of praying, I was amazed at God! Praying His will worked. God means what He says!

Praying God's will is praying for what He wants, not what I want. We both may have the same end in sight, but the way we get there is entirely up to God. He is allowing certain situations to take place because it is the way to Him! God was using where I fell short in my parenting and my son's own choices to work together for a glorious end. God used this long road to teach me how to abide in Him. He taught me more about prayer and hearing His voice. God used this far off, lonely road to bring my son home to Him! "For we know that

God causes all things to work together for good to those who love God, to those who are called according to His purpose" (Romans 8:28).

To pray God's will is to let go of control. We can actually block answers to our prayers by praying self-will prayers and being disobedient to what God's will is. In 1 John 5:14 we read, "This is the confidence we have in approaching God: that if we ask anything according to his will, he hears us." We can be confident asking God for anything that is according to His will and His Word. He says that He hears us, which means that He is *truly* listening! Keeping true to His character of a loving Father, He is listening to us with compassion. This means we can expect an answer to come.

God tells us in John 15:7 that, "If ye abide in me, and my words abide in you, ye shall ask what ye will, and it shall be done onto you" (KJV). If God's Word abides in us, and if we abide in Him, we are being renewed and changed to have the heart of God. We will be able to pray according to His will. This can happen because our self-will is surrendered, taken captive, and is given up. We have been changed at the heart level because now we have a new mind and a new way of thinking. We are thinking His ways and His desires so our prayers come from our newly-changed heart. Our desires change and line up with God's desires.

Abiding in Christ and His words abiding in us sanctifies the will. John 17:19 tells us to *"be sanctified through the truth"* (KJV). Having had our will sanctified, made holy or set apart for His purpose, we can ask what we will and it will be given to us. Our prayers are accommodating God, not God accommodating us. Our prayers become set apart for God's purpose. God's will does not change. Our prayers do!

If you are abiding in Christ, you are bearing fruit! One of those fruits is praying for others. One abides in Jesus through talking to Him and seeking Him through prayer and the Word. Jesus says to us in John 15:5, "I am the vine; you are the branches. If you remain in me and I in you, you will bear much fruit; apart from me, you can do nothing." As the believer grows and matures and spends more time alone with God, he is able to trust and wait on the Lord for His answers to prayer. Abiding brings fruit into our lives, but the fruit that God is talking about is fruit that is a blessing to others. The fruit of abiding in Him will be powerful prayers that get results in building His Kingdom and for His will to be done. This will include our family and others who are still on their way into the family of God. We do not want our prayers to be weak, but they will stay that way without truly abiding in Christ! Pressing on and pressing into God and abiding in Him, is what we need to do for prayers that win the lives of our lost loved ones.

Sometimes it is not always easy to recognize God's will. We have an enemy who has come to steal, kill, and destroy, us!! God's will doesn't always look the way we expect it to look. When Jesus died on the cross, it did not look like something that would be God's will, but it was part of a much larger picture! We must trust God. When things do not look like God's will, it could be God's grand plan at work! God's will is always to bring life, to restore and to save even when we can't see it. Keep abiding and keep praying.

The enemy will be out to deceive us and destroy us. However, there is another enemy which is hard to recognize and that is our own self-will and our own selfish desires. We try to manipulate God with our prayers to get answers to line up with what our hearts are seeking. Instead we need to allow God who knows what is best for us, who knows the big picture of our story, to bring answers to our prayers in His way, His timing and according to His will. The best way to pray for a miracle is to end each prayer with, "God Your will be done, for and in this situation." When you hand it over to Him, He straightens your prayer out to His will! Then His will... will be done!

Chapter 15

EVANGELIZE!

"...Go and bear fruit that will last." John 15:16

Kay Arthur, well-recognized Bible teacher, says that prayer is part of Kingdom building. If we pray, "thy Kingdom come," we are praying that God will prepare souls to receive Jesus. We are sent into all the world to preach the gospel of Jesus and to build His Kingdom. This is called the Great Commission. This world is reached through one soul at a time turning to Christ. Our prayers matter for expanding the Kingdom of God along with our going and making disciples! To make her point, she quoted a favorite pastor of hers, Adrian Rogers, who was faithful in doing this until his death.

> No matter how faithfully you attend church, how generously you give, how circumspectly you walk, how eloquently you teach, or how beautifully you sing, if you are not endeavoring to bring people to Jesus Christ, you are not right with God. We need to be right with God by doing what he has commanded us to do. (*Lord, Teach Me to Pray in 28 Days*, p.75-76)

God is "not willing that any should perish but that all should come to repentance" (2 Peter 3:9, NKJV). God is Sovereign and this is His will. God's purpose here on earth is to build His Church, and we are part of the building process. Others come to know Christ through our prayers and through the preaching of the gospel. Romans 10:1 says, "Brothers, my heart's desire and prayers to God for them is that they may be saved" (ESV). Romans 10:14 reads, " How, then, can they call on the one they have not believed in? And how can they believe in the one of whom they have not heard? And how can they hear without someone preaching to them?" Most prayers in the New Testament are for boldness to preach the gospel. "Pray for me... that I will fearlessly make known the mystery of the gospel" (Eph. 6:19). Our responsibility is to pray and preach. Dr. Jack Arnold, former president of Equipping Pastors International, says that prayer is "essential in the salvation of all who believe in Christ and without prayer no one will ever be saved... God has planned that certain events shall come to pass, but He has also decreed that these events shall come to pass through the means He has appointed for their accomplishment... Prayer is a means for carrying out the eternal purpose of God... Without prayer, nothing happens spiritually." (Arnold, Jack. "God's Sovereignty and Christian Prayer", www.monergism.com, PDF, Feb.2013) Pray for boldness for yourself and others. Pray for spiritual eyes to be opened! Pray!

Dr. John Davis, pastor and teacher at ICM College in Orlando, taught about the importance of evangelizing in order for our prayers to be heard. Evangelism comes with a promise. In John 15:16 we see this promise. "You did not choose me, but I chose you and appointed you to go and bear fruit—fruit that will last. Then the Father will give you whatever you ask in my name." No one can obey God and not get what is promised! We are to bear fruit which are souls for the Kingdom. Our prayers may be hindered because we do not evangelize and tell others about Christ. *Then, when you bear fruit, the Father will give you whatever you ask in my name.* So whatever you ask, you will get your answer.

It was exciting when I learned this because I do share the gospel message with others. Did the Father hear my prayers because of this? I think God was talking to me through John Davis. Understanding this truth has motivated and encouraged me to get going! If you need answers to prayer, get right with God by sharing the Good News of Jesus with those that are lost. Do not be afraid, God goes with you! Look at it this way: you "get to win a soul" for God!

In his book, evangelist Mark Cahill says to change your mindset on sharing Christ with others. He says that we don't pray because we got to, but get to. We don't read the Word because we have to, but we get to. We get to give back to God. "By the way, when we die, it is not that we have "got" to go to heaven, but we "GET" to go to Heaven. . . you get to share your faith with the lost. . . When you die and "GET" to go to Heaven, you get to bring as many people as you want to!" (*One Thing You Can't Do in Heaven,* p.26) I recommend this book and Mark Cahill's other book, *One Heartbeat Away.* Last fall, my 86 year old mother came for a visit. She picked out Mark Cahill's book from my shelf and could not put it down. When she went home, she took it with her and bought even more copies to give out to others. She is now asking people, "If you were to take your last breath, do you know if you would go to Heaven?" This is a great question because she lives in a retirement home and has witnessed many last breaths! Way to go, Mom! If my mother can ask this question, so can you.

In 2011, I participated in an amazing mission trip to evangelize the Island of Jamaica! It was called Cruise with a Cause and what a great experience, being with 3000 fired-up Christians. While we sailed to the island, my friend Jackie and I attended all the classes and concerts we could fit in. We went to two evangelism classes and one thing I remember the leader saying was, "Expect to be a little fearful because you are coming against the enemy!" The mission included going to 200 schools on the island to tell them about the Lord. The government invited us to come and provided us with tracts to give out and to get names for follow-up. Jackie and I signed up to visit one of the high schools and our leader turned out to be Anthony Evans, a Christian singer and the son of Dr. Tony Evans. We got to talk with him and his young band members on our hour-long bus ride to the school. The school teachers and students were so receptive. The trip also included a Christian concert with 40,000 in attendance where we prayed with people to accept the Lord. The last day we did street evangelism. The team effort included over 20,000 decisions for Christ!! For a majority of the people on this trip, it was their first time to pray with someone to accept Jesus as Lord and Savior! We were a team sharing the love of Christ!

Every Christian can be an evangelist by "going into their world" in their way. Every Christ follower is a minister and called to tell others about what Christ has done for them. Jesus has already done everything necessary for all people to have eternal life. They are just one decision away. Most do not even know they have a decision to make. I for one, did not know! I was 34 years old before I was told this through someone inviting me to a church where I heard the gospel message for the very first time. The sermon that day taught me about one of the attributes of God. God is a *just* God. A just God cannot allow sin into heaven so our *loving* God provided the cross as *the* way for our sin to be judged. Those who receive Jesus as Lord will not be judged for their sin. Until this day, I only thought of God as a loving God who would not send anyone to hell except for those who were *really* bad! I thought He graded on the curve! I lacked critical information and biblical truth although I knew *"about Jesus"* all my life.

We, who carry this life-saving message must tell them. Your style could be to invite them to church or a small group. You may be able to have the direct and bold approach like Peter. You may be the one who uses intellectual discussions. You may evangelize through your works of service, but you must make sure you "tell" them the Good News! Your way may be to build relationships first. You may have a platform to speak from like Tim Tebow did or you may use your music, art, dance, photography, or writing ability. Every Christian has a personal testimony to tell. This is a great way to share Christ because people like to hear stories they can relate to. Your story is the very best story someone needs to hear. It may be their rescue story! Another very simple way to share Christ is to just give out booklets like the "Our Daily Bread" devotional. Say, "Would you like a book?" Then just hand them one. You may become a tract minister, handing out tracts in your way. Just find a way and get your mind set on the fact that you have the most amazing and unbelievable news to share. People lack *critical* information! If *you* do not tell them, who will?

We are Christ's ambassadors and are given the awesome responsibility of bringing the message of reconciliation to others. Since we have been reconciled to God through Jesus, "He has committed to us the message of reconciliation. We are therefore Christ's ambassadors, as though God were making his appeal through us" (2 Co. 5:19b-20). Each Christian has been given this ministry of encouraging others to come to faith in Christ. In one of his sermons, Adrienne Rogers, says to win souls because we love Christ. Also, we do not want to go to heaven empty handed, but with a soul-winner's crown, for those we have won for Christ. There will be rewards in heaven and there will be regrets if all we do on earth is burned, having no eternal value. He called this being "singed, but saved." (Rev. 22:12, 1Cor.3:11-15, Phil. 4:1) Just start telling others your testimony and then get trained. What would you do if you got paid $1000.00 for every person you lead to Christ? Their eternal salvation is worth much more than this. ("The Soul Winners Six Mighty Motivations". Love Worth Finding Ministries, 2006. CD-ROM)

So that our Father will give you whatever you ask in Jesus' name, go save souls! Simply, share His love!

Chapter 16

PRAYERLESSNESS IS A SIN!

"As for me, God forbid that I should sin against the Lord in ceasing to pray for you."
(1 Samuel 12:23, KJV)

Taped to the side of a bookcase in my prayer closet (my bedroom nook) is the above verse. This is a reminder to me that not praying is a sin of omission and disobedience to God. Jesus said to never give up praying (Luke 18:1). The Word says to "Pray without ceasing" (1Thes.5:17, KJV). Prayer to the Christian is like breathing to the body. It is *life* to the believer . . . keeping in relationship to our Father in heaven. Darlene Bishop, Christian author, says that if Christians do not pray, they are carnal and they do not have anything exciting to talk about. They have no answers to prayer! She writes, "Prayerfulness makes you a bigger person, and prayerlessness makes you selfish." It is not good to be separated from God. "Devils know when you've been with Jesus, and they fear only those who pray. That means that only people who pray have power with God. This is why God's Word exhorts us: "Men ought always to pray, and not to faint." Luke 18:1. ...Prayerlessness is a serious sin that we need to deal with and overcome." (*Spiritual Desire,* p.72, 78)

Howard Hendricks says that struggling to pray is no accident. It is a serious deception by Satan. For 67 years as a Christian he has struggled in this area. He explains,

> Satan does not mind if you study your Bible. Just so you don't pray. You will become a smarter sinner, but you won't become like Jesus Christ.

You'll have more comprehension and more information, but not more transformation. Satan does not mind if you share your faith, just so you don't pray because he knows if you don't, that it is far more important to talk to God about men, than to talk to men about God. Satan does not mind if you become neurotically, compulsively active down at your local church or para-church, just so you don't pray. Because then you will be more active, but not really accomplishing anything of permanent value. ("Lessons from the Prayer Life of Jesus". Worship Forever! Moody Radio, 2010. CD-ROM)

If we are to become like Jesus, we must learn how to pray and have a real relationship with our Father like He did. Real change in us takes place through learning to pray. It is a process and a journey of great personal discovery. Satan does not want you to take this journey because you will have found the key to defeating him.

In the Bible, Jesus tells us what is better, being busy doing good things, or sitting at His feet. Martha complains that Mary is not helping her and Jesus replies, "Martha, Martha, you are worried and upset about many things, but only one thing is needed. Mary has chosen what is better, and it will not be taken away from her" (Luke 10:41-42). That is such an important statement, "only one thing is needed." Jesus did not say "recommended," but " needed." Martha was neglecting her Guest, putting chores ahead of Him. Her priorities were wrong and this is sin. Richard Halverson, former Chaplain of the U.S. Senate, states it like this, "You can organize until you are exhausted; you can plan, program, and subsidize all your plans, but if you fail to pray, it is a waste of time. Prayer is not optional for us. It is mandatory. Not to pray is to disobey God." (bishopfoleybeach.blogspot.com)

In his book, Pastor Bill Hybels says that "Authentic Christians have strong relationships with the Lord—relationships that are renewed every day. . . Embarrassingly few Christians ever reach this level of authenticity: most Christians are just too busy. . . .authentic Christianity is time. Not leftover time, not throwaway time, but quality time. Time for contemplation, meditation and reflection. Unhurried, uninterrupted time." Hybels suggests a way to slow down using a three-step program that works. Using a journal, first write for 10 minutes about what is going on in your life, second write down your prayers, and third, now that you have slowed down, listen to God. "Some people tell me they don't need to schedule regular time for prayer—they pray on the run. These people are kidding themselves." (*Too Busy Not to Pray,* p.100, 104)

Christian author, Jerry Savelle writes these life-altering words, "The quickest way to have your needs met is to get involved in the needs of others." (*Prayer of Petition*, p. 199) Praying is the most powerful way to help others. The Word says that you will reap what you sow, "Be not deceived; God is not mocked: for whatsoever a man soweth, that shall he also reap" (Gal. 6:7, KJV). Sow prayer and reap answers to prayer, but pray in line with God's Word. "With God all things are possible" (Matt. 19:26).

God does not want to hear our opinions, but He is looking for someone who will hear His heart. We need to be in His throne room, close to Him, to hear His heart. One time I had a vision of the Father taking my hand and placing it on His heart. He needs me to do this always! He is building a church and whatever we are asking for has to line up with what the Father is doing. He is looking for someone to pray His will in heaven down to earth, for someone who loves Him enough to enter His throne room, "to enter the Most Holy

Place by the blood of Jesus" (Heb. 10:19). He is looking for "a man . . .who will stand before me in the gap on behalf of the land" so He won't have to destroy it (Eze. 22:30). Jesus is asking for and looking for someone who will pray for those He gave His life for.

Will you be the someone or will our Father say, "But I found none" (Eze. 22:30b, KJV). Can He find you? Martin Luther says, "To be a Christian without prayer is no more possible than to be alive without breathing." (Roth, *Prayer Powerpoints,* p. 19) Christian, when you meet the Lord on that day, will He say to you, "Well done good and faithful servant!" (Matt. 25:21).

Chapter 17

PRAYING AND EXPECTING YOUR MIRACLE

"Ask, and it will be given to you; seek, and you will find; knock, and it will be opened to you: For everyone that asks receives; and he that seeks finds; and to him who knocks, the door will be opened." Matthew 7:7-8

If we pray correctly, we should expect to receive what we asked for. Andrew Murray explains that this is God's law! "Ask and you will receive; everyone who asks receives... This is the eternal law of the Kingdom. . . . If we ask and get no answer, it is because we have not learned to pray properly. ...There must be something in the prayer that is not as God would have it. We must seek guidance to pray so the answer will come." (*With Christ in the School of Prayer,* p. 40-41) I recommend reading books on how to pray because every time I pick up a book on this subject, God shows me something new that He wants me to know. I am in constant prayer "school."

Six years ago my prayers consisted of telling God about all my problems and needs which was not new information to Him! I knew two principles about prayer which were "ask" and "ask God." If God had more to add, I needed to know, because I needed prayers answered! I am amazed at how far God has brought me and taught me about this privilege and responsibility He calls prayer. It is actually getting exciting because He has told me that there is so much more He has to show me! We are going deeper yet!

Just last week, Germaine Hoffman, my anointed Bible study teacher said, "God does not have favorites, but He does have intimates." ("The Altar", Women's Bible Study, Mar. 26, 2013) I said, "God, I want to be one of your intimates!" In His Word He says, "You will seek me and find me, when you seek me with all of your heart, I will be found by you, declares the Lord" (Jeremiah 29:13-14a). The key is "with all of your heart." God will see your heart and honor your effort. He took my first small steps and turned them into one amazing miracle...my husband saved just in time!

Learning how to pray biblically is truly a journey but one that every Christian needs to be on. Author E.M. Bounds writes, "He does the most for God who is the highest skilled in prayer." (*Understanding Prayer,* p.12) The following are some prayer basics. Add the one or ones that you are missing in your prayer life. What is God saying to you? Get started on your personal journey with God and expect your miracle!

We must pray God's will. "Not my will but yours be done" (Luke 22:42). The Bible also says, "You ask and do not receive, because you ask amiss" (James 4:3, NKJV). If we are not asking for what is God's will, but rather for something for our own pleasures, this prayer cannot expect an answer. This is a self-centered prayer which has the wrong motive. The correct motive is that the Father be glorified. "Whatever you ask in My name, that will I do, so that the Father may be glorified in the Son" (John 14:13, NKJV). We must pray in submission to God's will lining up with His Word to pray properly. God loves us and wants our best which is His will for us.

We must pray in the Name of Jesus. The way that we are to approach God is to pray to the Father in Jesus' name. Jesus is our Mediator and Advocate between us and the Father. Jesus said, "And in that day ye shall ask me nothing. Verily,

verily, I say unto you, Whatsoever ye shall ask the Father in my name, he will give it you" (John 16:23, KJV). Jesus is sitting at the right hand of the Father "in that day" and tells us to ask Him nothing, but ask the Father in His name. We are able to pray to the Father because of what Jesus has done on the cross to open the way. We can come boldly into the throne room, not because of who we are, but based on who Jesus is and He is our Advocate. We have a restored relationship with God, through Jesus. We are to pray to the Father in Jesus' name.

We must have faith and believe. Matthew 21:22 says, "All things you ask in prayer, believing, you will receive" (NASB). You can only believe if you have a right picture of God and His character. Knowing of God's faithfulness, trustworthiness, kindness, compassion and goodness gives us faith to believe. If we have unbelief, we are shedding doubt on God's character. He is the God of "how much more" as we read in Matthew 7:11, "If you, then, though you are evil, know how to give good gifts to your children, how much more will your Father in heaven give good gifts to those who ask Him!" We must grow in faith by reading the Word because, "Faith comes by hearing, and hearing by the Word of God" (Romans 10:17, NKJV). Mark Hankins, pastor and author, heard the Lord say to him, "Some people are only one step away from a miracle." It may not be a difficult step, but one that lines up closer to God's way, power, and plan. He says, "the spirit of faith works by believing and speaking." (*The Spirit of Faith*, p.78, 79) Could your one step be *believe* or could it be *speak*? When you have faith and believe, then "speak to your mountain" it will move!

We must ask. Mark 11:24 says, "Therefore whatever you ask for in prayer, believe that you received it, and it will be yours." Charles H. Spurgeon tells us, "Whether we like it or not, asking is the rule of the kingdom." (*Prayer Power Points*, p. 22) Shepherd writes, "There is an undeniable correlation between asking God for miracles and receiving them." (*When You Need a Miracle,* p.31) That day I asked my Sunday school class to pray for a miracle for my son in Chicago, in God's time, I received an overdue, but right on time miracle! "You do not have because you do not ask God" (James 4:2b).

We must approach God boldly. In Hebrews 4:16 it says that we are to "draw near with confidence to the throne of grace, so that we may receive mercy and find grace to help in time of need" (NASB). We are not to come timidly, but we can come with confidence because of what was done on our behalf at the cross. "Therefore, brothers, since we have confidence to enter the Most Holy Place by the blood of Jesus, by a new and living way opened for us through the curtain, that is, his body" (Hebrews 10:19-20). Jesus' torn flesh removed the curtain so that all believers can come into God's presence in a new and living way. This new way is a real relationship with God and not a religious act. A.W. Tozer says that we have full assurance of faith through the veil that was torn and that we then can come with a boldness that is consecrated with the blood. We enter the "holiest place in the universe" standing in the presence of almighty God. God grants us to "come into the throne room" with a "confident expectation on what is going to happen next!" ("Prepare by Prayer". Worship Forever! Moody Radio, 2010. CD-ROM)) Come boldly expecting!

We must forgive others. We are commanded to forgive. Jesus said, "And when you stand praying, if you hold anything against anyone, forgive them, so that your Father in heaven may forgive you your sins" (Mark 11:25). If we have unforgiveness in our heart, we cannot get close to God. D.L. Moody said, "I firmly believe a great many prayers are not answered because we're not willing to forgive someone." (http://Christian-quotes.Ochristian.com) Gaspar Anastasi, Pastor of Word of Life Ministries, writes, "Unforgiveness is a sin and, like any other sin, it opens the door for Satan to wreak havoc in our lives. We can get sick in our spirit, soul and even our physical bodies because of it." We cannot forgive from our human nature but can only forgive "through faith from a born-again spirit." This is forgiving God's way, and is complete. You do not have to do it over and over again. (*Seven Steps to Complete Forgiveness,* p.1-8) Forgiveness is a decision, an act of the will.

We must be led by the Spirit. Romans 8:14 says, "For as many as are led by the Spirit of God, these are sons of God"(NKJV). We must live abiding in Christ and the Holy Spirit. Andrew Murray writes, "What our prayer achieves depends on what we are and what our lives are. Living in the Name of Christ is the secret of praying in the Name of Christ; living in the Spirit is necessary for praying in the Spirit." (*With Christ in the School of Prayer,* p. 189) The Holy Spirit comes when we have new life in Christ, and He is "the breath of God." The Holy Spirit connects the Son to the Father in prayer. "He is our Spirit of prayer. True prayer is the living experience of the truth of the Holy Trinity. The Spirit's breathing, the Son's intercession, and the Father's will become one in us." (*With Christ in the School of Prayer,* p. 191) When we pray, keep one ear tuned into the Spirit. Learn to listen and be led by the Spirit.

We must know that God is our Source. When we pray, we must truly believe that our prayers can change a situation or our prayers are meaningless and have no power. We must also know that God is the source of the power. "He is before all things, and in Him all things hold together" (Col.1:17). "Be strong in the Lord, and in the power of His might" (Eph. 6:10, KJV). "Commit to the Lord whatever you do, and your plans will succeed!" (Pr. 16:3). Our source is not others and it is not ourselves. "Now unto him that is able to do exceedingly above all we ask or think" (Eph. 3:20, KJV). He, God, is able. Jerry Savelle, pastor and author, says when praying, "never forget who your Source is. . . No matter what's going on around you, no matter what's happening in the natural, know that God is your refuge. He is your safe place. He has not forgotten your name. He has not forgotten your address. God has not forgotten how to do the miraculous on your behalf. He is your Source!" (*Prayer of Petition,* p.30) Bill Hybels strongly encourages us to do, "Whatever it takes for you to own the doctrine of God's omnipotence, do it. Until you own it, you will be a faint-hearted pray-er. You'll make a few wishes on your knees, but you won't be able to persevere in prayer until you know in your heart that God is able." (*Too Busy Not to Pray,* p.35) God will not just help with the answer, God is the answer! "I will even make a road in the wilderness!" (Isaiah 43:19, NKJV)

*****

To pray and get prayers answered, we must have fellowship with God. God is faithful, but are we? He tells us, "God is faithful, who has called us into fellowship with his Son, Jesus Christ our Lord" (1 Cor.1:9). Fellowship takes two, so who is missing? Praying is about relationship and there are different kinds of prayer that we can use and enjoy.

Different kinds of prayer include prayers of:

- **Praise**: where we focus on and praise Him for His greatness and who He is.
- **Thanksgiving**: for what God has done.
- **Confession**: agreeing with God where we have fallen short which is called sin!
- **Forgiveness**: for ourselves and for those we need to forgive. We cannot communicate with God until we pray this type of prayer. "Sometimes we only forgive enough to keep an open door, but we don't put the ax to the root of unforgiveness." (Ayers 53)

- **Petition**: asking God for a need for ourselves or another.
- **Agreement**: standing in faith with others.
- **Intercession**: prayer that starts with God for what He wants done in someone's life. He moves us to pray for them.

Prayers are meant to be answered. God has given man the power to put God to work to do His will. E.M. Bounds says it this way, "God has of His own motion placed Himself under the law of prayer, and has obligated Himself to answer the prayers of men. He has ordained prayer as a means whereby He will do things through men as they pray, which He would not do otherwise." God commands us to pray so that He can have His will come down to earth. "Prayer puts God's work in His hands, and keeps it there. . . . He highly esteems men of prayer." In every movement of God, prayer must precede it. For whatever is for God's cause He says "Ask Me and I will do it." (*Understanding Prayer,* p.133, 137-138) God wants to answer your prayer. He wants you to put Him to work on His project. Believe this, pray correctly, and get your miracle.

Chapter 18

SPIRITUAL WARFARE AND SPIRITUAL WEAPONS!

"For our struggle is not against flesh and blood, but against the rulers, against the authorities, against the powers of this dark world and against the spiritual forces of evil in the heavenly realms." Ephesians 6:12

When we are born, we enter a battleground, not a playground! There is an invisible war raging in the heavenlies. There are three heavens. When man looks up toward heaven at night, what is visible is the first heaven. God is in the third heaven. In between these two is the mid-heaven where Satan and his fallen angels war against man to do whatever they can to prevent God's purposes of mercy and grace to come to earth. The devil is angry, and he is your enemy. Since before you were born, Satan has been after your plan and purpose that God has for you. He has a customized scheme against you, and it usually starts in childhood or even at birth. He knows what works against you, and he has been using it! He blinds the minds of those who do not yet believe. He lies and makes sin look attractive, but it destroys you and your family. The Word says, "For we are not unaware of his schemes" (2 Cor.2:11b).

When you are born again, you enter a war zone! You are now dangerous to the enemy, but you fight from a position of victory in Jesus! You win, but you still have to fight the battles. We need to know our enemy and use our God-given weapons to defeat him. "For the weapons of our warfare are not carnal, but mighty through God to the pulling down of strongholds" (2Cor.10:4, KJV). Chip Ingram, pastor and teacher, says, "The fact that we were born in the middle of a war raging in the middle of an invisible world is not comforting news, but it is vital information. It impacts nearly every area of our lives, in fact, is the real arena in which we live. . . It is real, it is serious, and it is ultimate in its consequences. We are soldiers in the battle that matters most." (*The Invisible War*, p.37-38)

LOIS'S BATTLE WITH THE DEVIL

This invisible war became real to me when I found myself in the same room with the devil himself! Hello! My son Brian had been dealing with a spirit of fear for over a year and because of this, a book was recommended to me titled, *Liberating the Bruised*, by Joe Allbright. It was a book on deliverance and even included examples of multiple personalities and talked about SRA victims. (Satanic Ritual Abuse) I immediately told my friend Lois about this, because she was such a victim and was searching for help. She read the book and found a counselor three hours away. Lois contacted her and set up a three day session. Lois asked me to go with her, but said that they would not allow me to attend her session. The second time she asked me, I agreed and thought that while she was at her sessions, I could just read one of my many books. . . a little retreat! I felt the Holy Spirit telling me to go.

When we arrived at the church, the prayer minister said I could stay with them in the room for the beginning, for prayer. She knew I was the one who gave the book to Lois. She started to feel comfortable with me participating and said that I could stay as long as I agreed with what they were doing. Also, if I felt anything happening in myself, uncomfortable feelings, I should step out. I had read the book, so I was familiar with this deliverance ministry. I became an intercessory prayer warrior in the background for Lois and was given Scripture that I could use to pray against the enemy.

Lois had been satanically ritually abused by the Masons for most of her young life, starting at birth! She lived in a dark world and had more than 200 personalities which came about during each abuse. The first day the team prayed many prayers for healing and deliverance, and Lois made a lot of progress. She felt for the first time in her life she could actually see the world as bright. A dark veil had been lifted from her. This was so very encouraging to her. Later that day, we went back to the hotel, and then the prayer minister called and asked if we could come back that evening for another session. This was their ministry night at the church. We were very willing to go back and get more healing! However, after an hour, Lois was getting tired and her mind was not able to focus. The devil was taking advantage! The counselor then suggested that she rest and come back the next day.

As we were walking out, a demon manifested in her and started to talk. He said, "I knew you would give up." Lois's countenance changed as the demon manifested. The counselor had her sit down in a rocking chair as she went to get the pastor. The pastor, holding his Bible, continued to quote Scripture to the demon as the demon kept answering back in defiance, "The Mason bible is the only true bible!" The demon laughed at the pastor reading Scripture. He was arrogant and evil. He had my full attention!

Now, I first thought, "I am not going to let Lois drive the car." I went to her purse and got her keys. Then I thought, "What about the hotel room? What is going to happen? Will I be safe?" That is when my counselor, the Holy Spirit said, "He who is in you is greater than he who is in this world." Right!! My peace returned and my courage mounted! I was strengthened in my spirit and started to join in spiritual warfare, praying Scripture. I became bold and took authority as an ambassador of Christ! I felt strong against this defeated enemy. After twenty minutes of battle, the demon left her. Lois was released, and she was now herself. She said she could hear the devil talking through her.

Then as we were walking out of the church, Lois started going into different personalities. She became Steven, a seven year old boy, and went to the corner and put his (her) head up against the wall. Then she became Kathy, and I looked in her eyes, and I said, "This is not Lois." I was not leaving until Lois was back. I looked at her and repeated what the counselors had said, "Who are you? What's your name?" After a minute or so, Lois became herself and I then felt secure enough to drive back to the hotel.

That night I was in a head-on battle with the prince of this world. He is real and he can be defeated! I knew that God had a reason He wanted me to see and experience this as I was now introduced to what is called deliverance prayer ministry. I learned that a Christian cannot be possessed, but they can be oppressed by a demon. The prayer minister told me that this was not her usual case and that maybe once in five years she would witness a session like this. Well, I did not know why God put this in my life, but trusted that He wanted me to experience this for reasons He would reveal in my future.

We have to know how to fight the evil one so he does not get in and distract us from our relationship with God and our purpose. If demonic oppression is evident, and the enemy has gotten in, know that help is available. I realized that there had been two other situations in my past which were demonic oppression. These were people with whom I knew that something was not right, but at the time, could not identify what it was. One person had eyes that just looked empty and another person took on a different personality. Also, anytime there is an overreaction to a situation, something that is not usual or normal, it can be caused by demonic influence. For example, fits of rage are not normal. There is, however, also a warning that comes with this knowledge. We must not blame everything on the devil, because there is also a factor of our personal responsibility. We must learn and know the difference.

What causes demonic influence? Besides those who actually seek to get involved with demons, there are activities we engage in that we think are innocent, but are not. Some of these include: palm reading, Ouija boards, fraternity oaths, relaxation CDs (especially subliminal ones), acupuncture, karate and even yoga. However, sin is the most common way that Satan enters and influences a person's life. Pastor Chip Ingram writes, "Probably the most common cause of demonic influence is unresolved anger and bitterness. ...Many Christians are not aware that unresolved anger is an open door to demonic hosts." (*The Invisible War,* p. 171-172) Approximately 80% of the time that a deliverance is not successfully complete is because there is unforgiveness. Forgiveness frees you from the enemy's schemes.

After coming home from my trip with my friend Lois, I thought I had better reread the book, *Liberating the Bruised,* and become familiar with the prayers and steps suggested in it. As I was reading, I thought I would just pray the prayers myself . . . for me! After a few days, I had worked through the book and prayers of deliverance for myself and began praying for my three sons. I prayed for them to be released from any ancestral demons through my authority in Jesus Christ. I was very aware of the influence Satan had on them and their ancestors, so if I was now able to come against the enemy for them, I was going to do what I could. The process basically involves going to the Father in prayer, reaffirming your faith in Jesus Christ, repenting of any known sin, renouncing the works of the devil, and believing and resting in your deliverance. Follow-up to this is to get into the Word and renew your mind, stay in obedience to God, and spend time praying to God by yourself and with others. From then on, resist the devil by submitting to God.

WEAPONS OF OUR WARFARE

Perhaps you do not need a deliverance ministry, but everyone needs to use their spiritual weapons. Satan is real, and he is not quitting until his time is up. Satan sets up strongholds in people through lies and deception. Strongholds are in the mind and come from false beliefs. The Bible defines strongholds as an "argument or high thing that exalts itself against the knowledge of God" (2 Co. 10:5, NKJV). These strongholds will keep an unbeliever captive or a believer unable to grow spiritually or find their plan and purpose. One of Satan's primary weapons is deception, which builds the strongholds. Two ways in which the enemy can control a person's life are through unforgiveness and believing lies.

Carnal weapons are useless in spiritual warfare, "For the weapons of our warfare are not carnal, but mighty through God to the pulling down of strongholds" (2Cor.10:4, KJV). The weapons we are to use are spiritual and mighty through God; they destroy, tear down, and blast the strongholds. Dutch Sheets writes, "With this powerful, miracle working dynamite [God] behind our weapons, we can become demolition agents violently tearing down Satan's strongholds." (*Intercessory Prayer*, p.169) We are to know our enemy, his schemes, and our weapons. Christians are the ones who are to pick up these weapons and use them! No dropped swords and dragging shields allowed! Our number one weapon is prayer. Jack Hayford writes, "Prayer is an act of violence." (*Prayer is Invading the Impossible,* p. 18) Prayer is powerful. Think of prayer as using spiritual dynamite. To pray to get your miracle, you have to be armed and dangerous! It is time to suit up and pray up!

What Suit? Violent Prayer Weapons of War!

- **Knowing our identity in Christ.** The Word of God says that in Jesus Christ I am: God's child (John 1:12), Christ's friend (John 15:15), a citizen of heaven (Phil 3:20), included (Ephesians 1:13), adopted as His child (Ephesians 1:5). God wants you to know your new identity. There are over 200 Scriptures in the Bible telling us who we are. Satan's primary scheme is to make us question and doubt ourselves. The enemy tries to cast doubt, and this depowers you. Knowing your authority, that you are a member of a royal priesthood, filled with the Spirit and a walking temple of God, empowers you. It closes the door to Satan.
- **The full armor of God.** "Put on the full armor of God so that you can take your stand against the devil's schemes" (Eph. 6:11). Live by truth, righteousness, peace, faith, your salvation, the Word of God, and pray in the Spirit on all occasions. We put on the armor so that we might pray "with all kinds of prayers and requests...always keep on praying for all the saints" (Ephs.6:18). Chip Ingram explains, "It is important to remember that the armor is a description of how we are to live out a dynamic relationship with Jesus. This is a lifestyle, not a checklist. . . the product of weeks, months, and years of practice and cultivation. This is something we do, not a formula we recite." (*The Invisible War,* p.75) For example, you do not just put on shoes of peace, you live at peace all day long. Check to see if you are wearing your armor. How's your peace? Are the shoes in your closet? How is your faith in God? Is your shield dragging? Are you being transformed by the Word and are you speaking it? Did

you drop your sword? Christian warrior, get up, suit up; you are on a battlefield and fighting for your miracle!

- **The Word of God.** Jesus used the spoken Word to fight Satan. "It is written" (Matt.4:4,7,10). The Word of God is the sword of the Spirit, who speaks through us. We should memorize Scripture to be used by the Spirit. Derek Prince writes, "As long as anyone remains ignorant of the Word of God, ultimately, he or she will become prey to the devil." (*Secrets of a Prayer Warrior,* p.151) In Psalm 138:2, we read how His Word is above even His name. "For You have magnified Your word above all Your name" (NKJV).

- **Knowing your authority.** In Christ we have authority over Satan to "stand against the devil's schemes"(Eph. 6:11). We are able to, "Resist the devil and he will flee" (James 4:7). We are able to "not give the devil a foothold" (Eph.4:27). We have "authority to trample on snakes and scorpions and to overcome all the power of the enemy" (Luke 10:19).

- **Waiting on God**. Waiting on God shows trust in Him and devotion to Him. "Our soul waits for the Lord; He is our help and our shield" (Ps. 33:20, NASB). "Rest in the Lord and wait patiently for Him; do not fret because of him who prospers in his way, because of the man who carries out wicked schemes" (Ps.37:7, NASB). Waiting is a weapon. My favorite waiting verse is, "I say to myself, "The Lord is my portion; therefore I will wait for him" (Lamentations 3:24). Wait in His presence, and listen to what the Holy Spirit is telling you to do. Waiting is actively listening for His instructions. Don't react to the devil. Dutch Sheets writes, "God chooses the times and the terms of battle....Warfare is not a responsive reaction but responsible action. It must be born from obedience." (*Intercessory Prayer*, p. 147) Some of my instructions have been: "Go", "Praise Me", "Love him", "Repent", "Forgive her", "Pray with...", "Speak to", "Read this", "Be still", "Sit with Me", "Get up", "Finish it", "Pray to me; more, again, more, again..."

- **Peace**. Satan wants to steal your peace so God can't work. God says to "Be still and know that I am God" (Psalm 46:10). Let peace be the umpire of your soul. When you are not at peace, go to God and pray until you find rest in Him. Peace is a weapon against Satan. "And the God of peace will soon crush Satan under your feet. The grace of our Lord Jesus be with you" (Rom. 16:20). "Be anxious for nothing" (Phil. 4:6, NASB). It is a command. Jerry Savelle writes, "Worry has the power to choke God's Word from manifesting in your life." (*Prayer of Petition*. p. 224)
- **The Name of Jesus.** "O Lord, our Lord, how excellent is Your name in all the earth, who have set Your glory above the heavens!...You have ordained strength, because of Your enemies, that You may silence the enemy and the avenger" (Psalm 8:1-2, NKJV). When you praise the Lord's name you close the mouth of Satan! Using Jesus' name which we as Christians have been given authority to do, the enemy must bow. Phil. 2:10 confirms this, "That at the name of Jesus, every knee should bow in heaven and on earth and under the earth." Jesus' name is like wearing a badge! Make use of this against that devil.
- **The Blood of Jesus.** "They overcame him by the blood of the Lamb and by the word of their testimony" (Rev. 12:11, KJV). We overcome the enemy as we testify to what Jesus has done for us and through us. Satan was defeated at the cross when Jesus shed His blood for our sins! Testifying to what Jesus did for us is a powerful weapon. Testifying is applying the blood of Jesus over us, so the destoyer will not be able to overtake us and our families. This is what happened for

the Israelites, when during Passover, they spread the blood of the lamb around the doorposts. We read in Exodus 12:23, "...and when he sees the blood...the Lord will pass over the door and will not allow the destroyer to enter your houses to strike you" (ESV). Blood must be applied! Testify!

- **Persistence.** In Luke 18:1 we are commanded, "They should always pray and not give up." Derek Prince explains that sometimes the answer cannot come because of "satanic opposition in a kingdom in the mid-heaven set in direct opposition to all the good that God wants to do for us." (*Secrets of a Prayer Warrior,* p. 133) We must pray until the breakthrough comes. We must have intensity and not pray half-heartedly. Jehoash, the King of Israel was rebuked for his lack of intensity. Elisha told him to strike the ground with the arrows. Jehoash struck the ground three times and stopped. Elisha angrily said, "You should have struck the ground five or six times" (2 Kings 13:19). He received an incomplete victory. I did not want an incomplete victory. I drew three arrows on a note card representing my three sons with this verse on it. I placed it on my dresser to remind me that I need to keep praying for their complete victory! I pray that they walk in their plan and purpose and are great witnesses for the Lord. I pray that they know His love, and they love others with the love of Christ. I pray that they bring others into the Kingdom and become servant leaders and fulfill their call.

- **Humility.** Stay humble because pride and self-righteousness is an open door to the enemy. Also, do not criticize other Christians because this is what the enemy does...finds fault. Don't help him! Instead, encourage and pray for your fellow Christian soldiers. "For this cause we...do not cease to pray for you" (Col.1:9, KJV).

- **Praise.** Praising and worshipping the Lord is a weapon against our enemy. "At the very moment they began to sing and give praise, the Lord caused the armies of Ammon, Moab, and Mount Seir, to start fighting among themselves" (2 Ch. 20:22, NLT). Praise and worship is totally focusing on God and not on ourselves. Praise is powerful. Stormie Omartian, author of numerous books on prayer says, "It is the purest form of prayer...It exalts Him for who He is....praise welcomes His presence in our midst." (*The Prayer that Changes Everything,* p. 5) If He is in our midst, the enemy has nothing to do but leave!
- **Bind and Loose.** Matthew 16:19 says, "And I will give unto thee the keys of the kingdom of heaven: and whatsoever thou shalt bind on earth shall be bound in heaven: and whatsoever thou shalt loose on earth shall be loosed in heaven" (KJV). We believers here on earth have been given the authority to bind demons in the spiritual realm. For example, a person may be blinded by demons in his mind and cannot accept the gospel. We can bind this demon! We can also loose someone who is held captive or loose God's will into a situation. Whatever has already been bound in heaven, we can bind on earth. Whatever has been loosed in heaven, we can loose on earth.
- **Obedience.** "This day I call heaven and earth as witnesses against you that I have set before you life and death, blessings and curses. Now choose life, so that you and your children may live" (Deut. 30:19). Obeying God is choosing life, and disobeying God known as sin, opens the door to Satan and says, "Come on in!" Sin gives Satan legal access to you! Obedience enforces what Christ did on the cross, victory over the enemy of your soul. Obedience shuts the door on him. Bill Johnson writes that, "Biblical prayer is always accompanied by radical obedience. God's response to

prayer with obedience always releases the nature of heaven into our impaired circumstances."(*When Heaven Invades Earth,* p.58) What blessing is waiting for you on the other side of your obedience? My son Brian was at this crossroad when he backslid and opened the door to the enemy. Clifford, a friend and saint, drove across the state and took Brian in with him for two weeks. I remember talking to Clifford on the phone and hearing those miracle words, "Brian is choosing life." Thank you Brian, Clifford and Almighty God! To God be the glory forever and ever!

The enemy was defeated at the cross. Jesus took the victory. But Satan is still on the attack, "prowling around like a roaring lion, looking for someone he can devour" (1 Peter 5:8). We do not have to defeat the enemy again, but we must reinforce the victory. Our greatest re-enforcer is intercessory prayer. Author Dutch Sheets, writes, "All that we do in our praying intercession must be an extension of what Christ did through His work of intercession...we must release and enforce. What He provided for us, we must seize by faith with spiritual weapons." (*Intercessory Prayer,* p. 150-151) Jesus defeated Satan at the cross, and we enforce this victory through prayer. Chip Ingram says that, "Intercessory prayer is our most powerful and strategic corporate weapon in spiritual warfare." (*The Invisible War,* p. 157) This is God's battle plan. "His work empowers my prayers, and my prayers release His work [at the cross]". (Sheets, *Intercessory Prayer,* p. 45)

Prepare Ahead!

A.W. Tozer says, "Battles are lost before they are fought! Battles are won before they are fought!" ("Prepare by Prayer". Worship Forever! Moody Radio, 2010. CD-ROM) The outcome is all in the preparation. You must prepare for spiritual battles through prayer. Jesus won the battle at the cross through prayer as He agonized all night in the Garden before the soldiers took Him. He told His disciples to "pray so that you will not fall into temptation" (Luke 22:46). Instead, they slept and all of them later deserted Him because they did not prepare through prayer. In his sermon, "Prepare by Prayer", A.W. Tozer says that, "Anticipatory prayer is the most effective preparation known to man in heaven and earth. It is the power and source of energy...Jesus prayed until He passed 'the cosmic crisis'." Christ knew that it was the Father's will that He drink the cup and go to the cross. When you know something is God's will and want to see it come to pass in your life, prepare by prayer.

When my husband was baptized that night in our church, it was God's will, and it was prepared by prayer. When my son, Brian, chose life after a setback and when he gave his life to the Lord in a rehab in Mississippi, it was God's will, prepared ahead by prayer. When my son, Colin, got down on his knees and turned his life over to the Lord, it was God's will, and prepared ahead by anticipatory prayer. When Shane went forward and rededicated his life to the Lord, it had been prepared by prayer. These battles were won before they were fought! It was prayer that brought God's power into the battle for their souls. In one of my favorite books, Tommy Tenney wrote, "...if your enemy is the King's enemy, then your battle is the King's battle." (*Finding Favor With the King,* p. 144) We and God have the same enemy, and our part is to pray, "Thy

Kingdom come." When we pray as God taught us to pray, then "His world collides with the world of darkness, and his world always wins." (Johnson, *When Heaven Invades Earth,* p. 63)

Prayer is the Christian's mighty weapon. William Cowper, a great hymn writer, wrote in one hymn, "Satan trembles when he sees the weakest saint upon his knees." In a chapter titled, "Battle On", Michael Catt, author, discusses warfare praying and writes, "If we are who we're supposed to be, Satan will oppose us. He doesn't bother those saints who don't bother him. He will leave the prayerless believer alone. But when we are actively engaged with God in prayer, we become noticed in dark, devilish places." (*The Power of Persistence,* p.157) God and I were on a rescue mission. I did not care how dark it got, Satan was not going to have my family! I battled from my knees. God trained me in prayer combat and God's mission was accomplished! Heaven invaded earth! Miracles arrived! God is glorified! Amen and Amen!

CONCLUSION

A few months ago, I attended a Rick Pino concert at a local church here in Fort Myers. I went because my son Shane's roommate was a very close friend of Rick's. As I left the concert, I felt very blessed because of one song. When Rick sang his song, "Pioneer", I heard my journey with God in those lyrics. The song described exactly how I have felt many times. I am a pioneer traveling into a frontier with the Lord. My sons and others are following, and because I go ahead, they will do much more for God than me. I realized that we are all pioneers, each with our own frontier as we press into our relationship with God. The song inspired me to think of this journey forward as an awesome adventure! Following are the lyrics to "Pioneer":

Pioneer, Pioneer
Keep pressing onwards beyond your fears
And only your Father goes before you to your own frontier
You're a Pioneer.
Uncharted wilderness stretches before you
And you thrive on going where no one has gone
Still it gets lonely when darkness rears
So sing by the fire until the dawn.
You travel light and you travel alone
And when you arrive nobody knows
But your Father in heaven, He is glad you can go
Cause those who come after you will need the road.
And what you have done, others will do
Bigger and better and faster than you
But you can't look back, you gotta keep on pressing through
There's a wilderness pathway and it's calling you.
Calling you, calling you

Keep pressing onwards beyond your fears
And only your Father goes before you to your own frontier
You're a Pioneer
(Pino) Listen at http://www.songlyrics.com/rick-pino/pioneer-lyrics

Prayer is the responsibility of every Ambassador of the Kingdom of God. Believer, that means you! When God gives you a burden, pray His will to earth. God's will is that you pray. Prayer creates intimacy between you and God. People ask, "What is God's will for my life?" As you start with prayer, He will further reveal His will for you. His will is that you abide in His Word. His will is that you pray biblically. His will is growing in intimacy with Him as you go on a personal journey with Him. Like me, you will have a season of personal discovery as you travel into your frontier; places you and God have not yet gone together. Every Christian still has a frontier to pioneer with God. Others will follow because you journeyed ahead. Others need your prayers. The most valuable thing we can do in our Christian walk is to partner with God in prayer, to bring His will to earth. On your journey you will learn to pray and receive a miracle like I did. Expect your miracle! Do it for God! Do it so that He may be glorified!

****

ARE YOU 100% SURE YOU ARE GOING TO HEAVEN?
ACCEPT JESUS CHRIST AS YOUR LORD AND SAVIOR!

****

Jesus replied, "I tell you the truth, unless you are born again, you cannot see the Kingdom of God." John 3:3 NLT
If you confess with your mouth, "Jesus is Lord," and believe in your heart that God raised him from the dead, you will be saved. Romans 10:9

Refer back to page 29, pray to make Jesus your Lord and receive your very own personal MIRACLE of eternal life!

References

Allbright, Joe. Liberating the Bruised.
    Spring, TX: Smooth Sailing Press, 2011. Print
Anastasi, Gaspar. Seven Steps To Complete Forgiveness.
    Freeport, NY: Word of Life Ministries, 1999. Print.
Arnold, Jack. "God's Sovereignty and Christian Prayer",
    www.monergism.com (PDF.) Feb.2013.
Arthur, Kay. Lord, Teach Me to Pray in 28 Days. Eugene, OR:
    Harvest House Publishers, 2008. Print.
Alves, Elizabeth. Becoming a Prayer Warrior. Ventura, CA:
    Regal Books, 1998. Print.
Batterson, Mark. The Circle Maker. Grand Rapids, MI:
    Zondervan, 2011. Print.
Banks, James. The Lost Art of Praying Together. Grand Rapids,
    MI: Discovery House Publishers, 2009. Print.
Bevere, John. Driven by Eternity. New York, NY: Warner Faith,
    2006. Print.
    —. Rescued. Bloomington, MN: Bethany House Publishers,
    2006. Print.
Bishop, Darlene. Spiritual Desire. Denver, CO: Legacy
    Publishers International, 2005. Print.
Bounds, E.M. Understanding Prayer. Uhrichsville, Ohio:
    Barbour Publishing, 2013. Print.
Cahill, Mark. One Thing You Can't Do In Heaven. Rockwall,
    TX: Biblical Discipleship Publishers, 2005. Print.
Catt, Michael. The Power of Persistence. Nashville, TN: B&H
    Publishing Group, 2009. Print.
Cooke, Graham. "The Art of Thinking Brilliantly". Vancouver,
    WA: Brilliant Book House, 2011. CD-ROM.
Copeland, Germaine. Prayers That Avail Much. Tulsa, OK:
    Harrison House, Inc., 1997. Print.
Daugherty, Billy Joe. "Praying Your Family Into Heaven!". Tulsa,
    OK: South Lewis Victory   Christian Center, 1993. Print.

Davis, John. "The Blood Covenant." International College of Ministry. Live-Web class, Orlando, FL. 5 February 2013. Lecture.
Enloe, Tim. Want More? Wichita, KS: EM Publishers, 2004. Print.
Evans, Dr. Tony. "Intimacy with God". Spiritual Life Conference, 2012. Dallas, TX. Conference speaker. Theological Seminary Chapel. podcast. http://www.youtube.com/watch?v=APH3HVckbsw
Franklin, Jentezen. Right People, Right Place, Right Plan. New Kensington, PA: Whitaker House, 2007. Print.
—-. Right People, Right Place, Right Plan, Devotional. New Kensington, PA: Whitaker House, 2008. Print.
Gothard, Bill. The Power of Crying Out. Sisters, OR: Multnomah Publishers, 2002. Print.
Gass, Bob and Debby. The Word for You Today. Alpharetta, GA: Evangelistic Association, Inc. Nov. 23, 2009. Print.
Hankins, Mark. The Spirit of Faith. Alexandria, LA: MHM Publications, 2007. Print.
Hendricks, Howard. "Lessons from the Prayer Life of Jesus." Worship Forever! Moody Radio, 2010. CD-ROM.
Hoffman, Germaine. "The Altar". Women's Bible Study. First Assembly of God, Fort Myers, FL., March 26, 2013. Teacher.
Hybels, Bill. Too Busy Not to Pray. Downers Grove, IL: InterVarsity Press, 1988. Print.
Ingraham, Chip. The Invisible War. Grand Rapids, MI: Baker Books, 2006. Print.
Jacobs, Judy. Stand Strong. Lake Mary, FL: Charisma House, 2007. Print.
Johnson, Beni. The Happy Intercessor. Shippensburg, PA: Destiny Image, Publishers, Inc., 2009. Print.
Johnson, Bill. When Heaven Invades Earth. Shippensburg, PA: Destiny Image Publishers, Inc., 2003. Print.

Liardon, Roberts. Greater Wiser Stronger; God Wants You to Increase! Laguna Hills, CA: Embassy Publishing Co., 2000. Print.

Matz, Duane. "The Devil Owns the Fence." The Daily Duvotional: Sunday, October 2, 2011. Web. http://todayslivingword.blogspot.com/2011/10/devil-owns-fence.html.

Mississippi Mass Choir. "It Was Worth It All". Album: Not By Might, Nor By Power. 2005. www.youtube.com/watch?v=iMAMvlkOfSc

Murray, Andrew. With Christ in the School of Prayer. New Kensington, PA: Whitaker House, 1981. Print.

Nee, Watchman. Burden and Prayer. Anaheim, CA: Living Stream Ministry, 1993. Print.

Omartian, Stormie. The Prayer that Changes Everything: Book of Prayers. Eugene, OR: Harvest House Publishers, 2005. Print.

Pino, Rick. "Pioneer." Album: The Narrow Road. Genre: Rock. http://www.songlyrics.com/rick-pino/pioneer-lyrics

Platt, David. Follow Me. Carol Stream, IL: Tyndale House Publishers, Inc., 2013. Print.

Prince, Derek. Secrets of a Prayer Warrior. Grand Rapids, MI: Chosen Books, 2009. Print.

Quillin, Rachel. The Christian Quote Book. Uhrichsville, OH: Barbour Publishing, Inc. 2004. Print.

Rogers, Adrienne. "The Soul Winners Six Mighty Motivations". Memphis, TN: Love Worth Finding Ministries, 2006. CD-ROM

Roth, Randall D. Prayer Powerpoints. Wheaton, IL: Victor Books/ SP Publications, Inc., 1995. Print.

Savelle, Jerry. Prayer of Petition. Ventura, CA: Regal, 2011. Print.

Sheets, Dutch. Intercessory Prayer: How God Can Use Your Prayers to Move Heaven and Earth. Ventura, CA: Regal Books, 1996. Print.

Shepherd, Linda Evans. When You Need a Miracle. Grand Rapids, MI: Revell/Baker Publishing Group, 2012. Print.

Sorge, Bob. Secrets of the Secret Place. Kansas City, MO: Oasis House, 2001. Print.

Stone, Perry. Opening the Gates of Heaven. Lake Mary, FL: Charisma House, 2012. Print.

Tchividjian, Tullian. Do I Know God? Colorado Springs, CO: Multnomah Books, 2007. Print.

Tenney, Tommy. Finding Favor with the King. Grand Rapids, MI: Bethany House, 2003. Print.

The River at Tampa Bay Church. http://www.revival.com/soulwinning-tools.24.1.htm

Tozier, A.W. "Prepare by Prayer". Worship Forever! Moody Radio, 2010. CD-ROM.

Williams, Grant. "Offenses Will Come". First Assembly of God. Fort Myers, FL, June 24, 2007. Sermon.

Made in the USA
Charleston, SC
18 March 2016